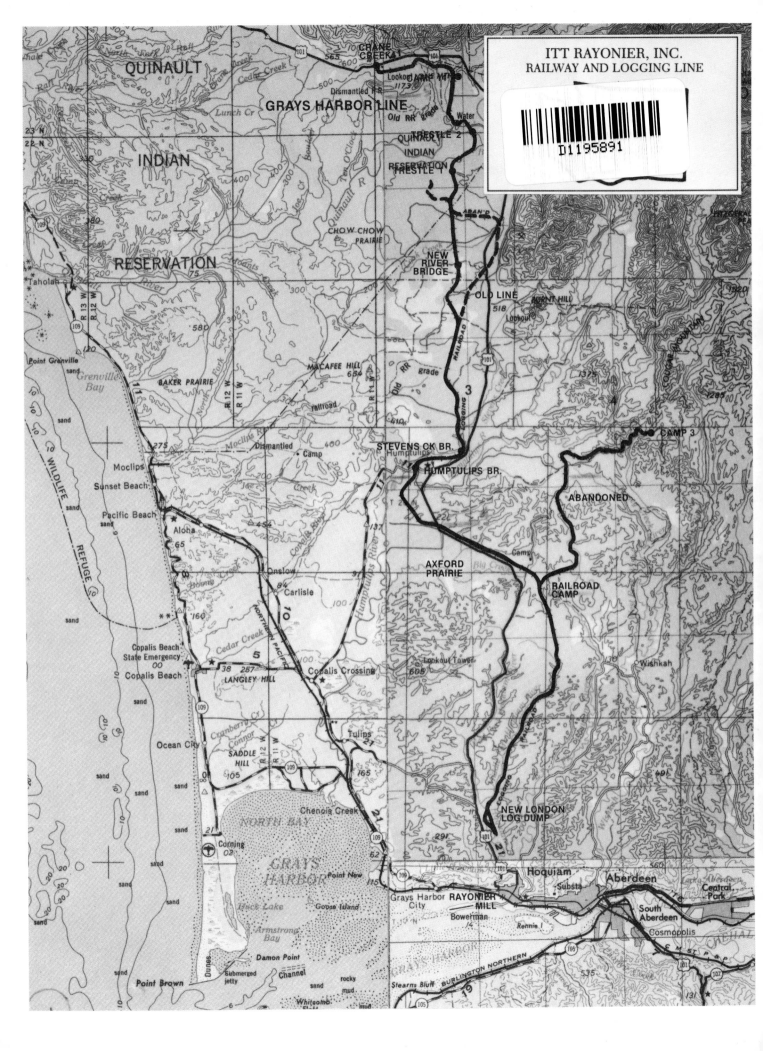

ITT RAYONIER, INC.
RAILWAY AND LOGGING LINE

D1195891

Rayonier

By James Spencer

Heimburger House Publishing Company
7236 W. Madison Street
Forest Park, Illinois 60130

Library of Congress Number: 97-75112
ISBN: 0-911581-46-6

Acknowledgements

I wish to thank Jay Fredricksen, public affairs manager of ITT Rayonier, and Roy Peacher, retired personnel manager, who assisted immeasurably in assembling the history of Rayonier. John Labbe, noted historian and author of many logging books himself, gave many hours of dialogue and research advice. Denny Ross, model builder, historian, and collector of railroad lore, also contributed much material. Photos from the collections of Ken Schmelzer and Al Farrow grace many of these pages. The heretofore unpublished photos from turn-of-the-century glass plates of H.G. Nelson were expertly reproduced by historian, collector and Rayonier photographer, Bill Jones.

The personal interviews were a particular pleasure: Alex McClean "Mac" Polson, nephew of Alex Polson; trainmaster Paul Pauly; Buster Corrigan, engineer; and Bob Hattan, crane operator, hostler and jack-of-all-trades. Thanks go also to Dave Skagen, locomotive engineer; Bill Roney, project engineer at Pacific Car & Foundry; Rayonier's Les Rowe, and retired timber division manager George V. Lonngren; to the many others who gave of their time and knowledge; and last, but far from least, my wife, Barbara. *Jim Spencer*

In this revised edition, a special thanks to Pete Replinger, who revised the text and supplied the diesel roster as well as new black and white and color photographs. *Don Heimburger, Publisher*

Table of Contents

Introduction

In the magnificent wilderness of northwestern Washington State the vast Olympic rain forest yields one of the largest, most majestic timber stands in all the world. Mountain after mountain, canyon after canyon, no slope is without its dense carpet of green. From this rich peninsula comes high-grade cedar, spruce and Douglas fir—some of the finest in the world.

As civilization reeled from England's great Industrial Revolution, it seemed everyone on the American continent was heeding the advice of Horace Greeley: "Go west, young man!" Towns and factories sprang up as fast as men could build them—and they just couldn't build them fast enough. A cry rang out across the land for more lumber. A speedier, more efficient method of getting felled trees out of the woods was sorely needed, and railroads provided the answer. Thus came the band of rugged men who surveyed the land and laid out a vast network of rails through the forests. The terrain was tough; the earth wet and slippery; the weather cold. Railroading was in its infancy and, in the case of logging operations, the need was there but the technology was not. The task was to develop and build equipment that could carry tons of wet wood on rough track and tight curves. Locomotives were needed with the power to climb steep grades and the braking capability to get safely down again. The challenge brought forth giant names in railroading history — Shay, Porter, Baldwin, and others. With ingenuity and enterprise they designed and built the equipment to meet the unique requirements of harvesting the Pacific Northwest timber.

To the pioneers of the late eighteenth century, timber was gold, and one of the biggest logging shows in the entire area began when, in the early 1900s, a fellow named Alex Polson came onto the scene. He built the Polson Brothers Logging Company into an empire which later became part of ITT Rayonier. As the company grew it acquired an impressive array of steam-powered equipment and a manpower force which defied the Great Depression, two world wars, and the rigors of survival in the forest. The Polson outfit was finally sold to Rayonier in 1948 and the new owners continued to add to the equipment roster.

Things are different, though, since steam has died. Diesels now ply the main line at ITT Rayonier, and most of the early logging spurs have gone the way of the old "slobber-stacks" and wood burners. But the memory lives on, and this book is dedicated to those pioneering men and machines, and to the industry they created.

When Alex Polson arrived in Washington this is the kind of timber he found. Later he would build a railroad through here to haul the "sticks" out to a lumber-hungry world. (H.G. Nelson photo, Rayonier collection)

Above, a team of engineers surveys what would soon become a new Polson brothers logging spur. (H.G. Nelson photo, Rayonier collection)

At right, a train of empty skeleton cars awaits the climb into the majestic timber stand of Washington's Olympic Peninsula. (Ken Schmelzer collection)

4

Camp 7.
Polson Logging Co
Hoquiam Wa 562
Nelson

In the days when steam shovels were actually powered by steam, crews work on the line at Camp 7. Note that the arm of this Bucyrus-Erie shovel is made of wood and that the railroad ties are rough-hewn and not ballasted. (H.G. Nelson photo, Rayonier collection)

Alexander Polson. (H.G. Nelson photo, Willliam D. Jones collection)

Chapter One
The Search for Gold

Down through the ages many a young man has set out to make his fortune in one field, only to wind up doing something completely different, and Alex Polson was an example. The son of Scottish parents in Nova Scotia, Canada, he rejected the prospect of a life on the farm in his parents' footsteps. No, Alex longed for gold! Lured by the prospect of adventure and instant riches, he struck out for the gold fields of the West at the ripe age of twenty-one. In 1876 he arrived in Deadwood in the Dakota territories, green, but eager to make his fortune. His luck, however, was like that of many other young men with thoughts of gold dancing in their heads. After months of fruitless digging, he was not rich—only tied, dirty and practically broke. Then came a close brush with disaster. Polson nearly purchased a salted mine—a worthless site planted with a little gold by an unscrupulous seller — which surely would have wiped him out altogether. Angry and disgusted, he finally went to work for a Deadwood lumber dealer. Although lumber was interesting work that enabled the young man to get back on his feet financially, he was again struck with gold fever after hearing tales of big strikes out in Carson City. He packed his gear and headed for Nevada, where he bought a small claim with his lumber earnings, but was taken again. This time he'd been suckered into a played-out mine that yielded only a smattering more than the Dakota mine would have.

Carson City was a boomtown. Rapid building brought about an acute need for lumber, and Polson, sensing money to be made, retired his pick and shovel and took a job at a local mill, later buying a partnership. One might think that a few years of success in Carson City would prove that lumbering offered a better, steadier life than taking chances on glory holes, but the adventurous Polson just couldn't seem to brush off the gold dust. Once again he was packing mining gear, heading this time for Tucson, Arizona — and to the same empty holes he had found before. That cured him. No more wild dreams and empty claims. If money was to be made, it was in lumber.

The West was the land of opportunity and people were moving to the Pacific Coast in droves. While in Deadwood and Carson City, Polson heard the loggers tell of giant stands of virgin timber on the Olympic peninsula of Washington—trees so big you couldn't get a saw large enough to cut through them! So in the spring of 1879 he packed his saddlebags and set out on horseback for Washington and, finally, for his real fortune. In Yakima Polson hired out as a log driver for an outfit that was cutting timber for the new Northern Pacific Railway, and the following year he moved to Olympia to work for the Ames Brown Company. In a short time Alex became a foreman for the company and not only inaugurated new methods for handling the huge Douglas fir, but also invented several items to make work easier and safer for the loggers in the woods. In fact, his work was so valued that his boss quickly dispatched him to oversee a new dam project for a friend.

Meanwhile, in 1881 two partners, Harvey Emerson and "Captain" Simpson, bought a vast tract of land at the mouth of the Hoquiam River, where they built a large sawmill and established a townsite. Word of Polson's knowledge and abilities spread quickly and the following year they invited him to come to Grays Harbor to construct a dam. Alex realized the potential for wealth in the Grays Harbor area so he sent for his brother Robert, and the Polson Brothers Logging Company was born.

The company was destined to become the greatest logging show of its time in the Pacific Northwest. The Polsons were clearly the do-ers, the innovators, and they became successful almost overnight. Even without the benefit of steam power their operation was producing some 250,000 shingles per day.

Thanks to their innovations and ability to diversify, they became one of the largest dealers of loggers' supplies and equipment, in addition to their shingle production. The Polson Brothers took a major step forward when they created the Hoquiam Timber Company, specializing in buying timberland, and it wasn't long before the brothers owned a large portion of the stands north of Grays Harbor.

The tedious practice of skidding logs with oxen frustrated the Polsons. As loggers worked their way deeper into the forest, the distance to the river increased, slowing the process even more, so they began considering the steam locomotive and steam donkey for this task. The brothers were among the first to fully utilize steam in the woods. They laid rail—in some cases, directly over the skid roads—into the forest and used steam skidders. The skidder was a large logging machine which used both winches and pulleys to move cut logs. Unlike the donkey, whose cables were attached to a spar tree, the skidder had its own tower for blocks and cables. Some skidders were mounted on their own wheels, while others had to be attached to huge sleds, as the donkeys were. With the aid of steam, monthly tallies increased and rails were driven deeper into the woods. As the logging operations grew, so did the need for equipment, and Alex Polson instructed his men to acquire anything they could to move out the timber. More track was laid, then came additional locomotives, donkeys and skidders, plus loaders to hoist logs up onto the newly acquired skeleton cars. The skeletons basically consisted of a massive steel or wood "backbone" running the length of the car, with a pair of chocks at each end to prevent the bottom row of logs from rolling off. These cars were much safer than the old "disconnects," which used the logs themselves to connect separate sets of trucks and had no air brakes. With the new equipment the operation became much more efficient. By the early 1920s 55 miles of railroad had been installed north of Hoquiam. Equipment included nine locomotives and at least 31 donkey engines. At last, Alex Polson had discovered his gold mine!

The story of Rayonier is not just the story of the Polson brothers, however. Another important figure in Rayonier's history was Edward Mills, a self-made man who began work at the tender age of 10 as a lawyer's apprentice stenographer in his native Wales. Mills arrived in America as a young man and settled in the Midwest, penniless and without any trade other than the smattering of legal knowledge he had picked up on his former job. But he was clever and quick to learn, and later secured a position at Price Waterhouse & Company. Young Mills studied every book he could get his hands on, then joined Peabody-Houghteling, a Chicago investment firm. Among Peabody-Houghteling's accounts was a couple of Canadian brothers, George and James Whalen. They operated three pulp mills in British Columbia at Fort Alice, Wood Fibre, and Swansons Bay, then decided to open another at Port Angeles, Washington. The operation was christened the Olympic Power and Paper Company and, with Peabody-Houghteling funds, equipment was purchased and moved to the new site. The brothers soon ran out of money, however, leading Peabody-Houghteling into receivership. In 1920 the firm dispatched Mills to recover lost capital from the Whalens and another failing project at the nearby Elway Dam, but the effort came too late. Mills had barely arrived at the site when he received word that the company had gone belly-up. Finding himself out of work, he decided to stay in Washington, hoping to find a better life.

Before Mills set out from Chicago, the desperate Whalens had sought financial relief from Isadore Zellerbach, one of the great pioneers of the paper industry. At that time Zellerbach was fighting desperately to retain a stronghold in the paper market, which had just been severely jeopardized when Crown Paper Company suddenly removed him as a distributor, despite a 20-year contract he had arranged for supplying pulp to *The San Francisco Chronicle*. Zellerbach sent his son Harold to inspect the Whalens' project; Harold was unimpressed with their operations, but nevertheless recommended that his father buy the equipment. Mills entered at an opportune moment. He cleverly packaged the holdings of Olympic Power and Paper together with the Elwah Dam project and sold it to Zellerbach, who named it the Washington Pulp and Paper Company, and assigned Mills as its manager. This merger was a milestone. It not only inaugurated Zellerbach's entry into paper manufacturing, but it brought together the men who would eventually create Rayonier, Incorporated.

Not content just to run a mill, Edward Mills contacted financier John Higgins and Senator Mark Reed, who was also manager of the Simpson Logging Company. The resourceful Mills was concerned about the vast waste created when potentially valuable wood cellulose was routinely sent to the furnace, and he needed financing to research a way for this waste to be converted into a gain. After much testing it was clearly determined that the waste could indeed be converted into valuable pulp. He convinced the two that a pulp mill could be built on Simpson's land at Shelton, using waste slabs and reject hemlock from Simpson's new reed mill as well as a new McCleary Timber Co. mill located on adjacent land. As a result, Rainier Pulp and Paper Company was incorporated in 1926, with Mills as president. Basking in the new operation's instant success, the three once again pooled their resources and formed the Grays Harbor Pulp Company. Another expansion, this time with a large investment by the Hammermill Paper Company of Erie, Pennsylvania, led to the Grays Harbor Pulp and Paper Company, and close on its heels, the Olympic Forest Products Company was formed in 1930 when Mills paid a visit to the S.D. Warren Paper Company in Maine. Mills now headed three successful companies, employing more than a thousand people. These three companies were eventually to become Rayonier, Incorporated, yet a few years would pass before they would actually become one.

In the meantime another exciting development was taking place. Just prior to the Civil War a budding chemist named George Audemars opened the door to formulating "artificial silk" from nitro-cellulose. After years of testing and perfecting, the product came into its own in 1924 when Kenneth Lord coined the word "rayon," the first of the manmade fibers. By the time the Washington Pulp and Paper Company was formed, rayon had become one of the unparalleled success stories of all time.

The Great Depression greatly curtailed paper and pulp production and it was clear to Edward Mills that if he were to survive, he needed badly to diversify. Instinct led him to the cellulose industry. He gathered samples of pulp from the Rainier plant at Shelton and sent them to the DuPont Company for examination. In 1931, with DuPont backing, Rainier started producing a dissolving pulp of consistent quality. This new wood pulp was called "Rayonier," coined by combining the names rayon and Mt. Rainier.

By the mid-30s Mills' companies were the leaders, both in production and technical proficiency. But as the early '30s brought about the need for diversification, the opposite was true later in the decade—it was time to simplify the tangled relationships and parallel activities of Rainier, Grays Harbor and Olympic Forest Products. Mills, president of all three, proposed a merger; 1937 saw the melding of the three companies and Rayonier, Incorporated was born on November 2. Rayonier prospered under Mills, acquiring numerous holdings throughout the United States and increasing its production immensely. Mills experienced increasingly tense relations with the company, however. By 1944, after considerable conflict over moving the corporate headquarters to New York, he was voted out of office. His problems compounded by ill health, he retired, and succumbed in 1949.

Upon Mills' retirement Isadore Zellerbach's son James took over temporarily as Rayonier's executive vice president, but due to his prior commitment to his father's company, he arranged for Edward Bartsch of the Chase Bank to take over Rayonier, Incorporated. Bartsch assigned Vice President Clyde Morgan to buy more holdings, and the years 1945 through 1947 saw Rayonier acquire the holdings of the Bloedel-Donovan Lumber Company and the Ozette Railroad—prior to this, Rayonier owned only mill sites. The real prize—the purchase that would unquestionably make Rayonier king—was the Polson Brothers Logging Company. Morgan, Martin Deggellar, and Rayonier worked diligently to that end, and the transaction was completed in 1948. That put Rayonier on the map. It now held nearly 400,000 acres of prime timberland, several billion board feet of timber and one of the largest logging railroad empires in the Pacific Northwest. The Polson Brothers Logging Company became history, and a new era was underway.

In 1950 William Reed, the son of Senator Mark Reed and then president of Simpson Logging Company, assumed temporary leadership of Rayonier under the title of executive vice president. A few months later, he was voted out by the board of directors and Clyde Morgan was elected Rayonier's new president in July of 1951. As Rayonier's vice president in the '30s, Morgan had been in charge of the Fernandina Mill in Florida. He continued building Rayonier's holdings and in 1954 acquired Alaska Pine, renaming it Rayonier Canada, Ltd. in 1959. (Many years earlier the same firm had been influential in Edward Mills' decision to go west—it used to be the old Whalen Brothers' operation.) By 1962 Rayonier had reached 843,000 tons of production, nearly doubling its output in 10 years. ITT Rayonier, Inc., came into being in April 1968 through the merger of Rayonier, Incorporated and The International Telephone and Telegraph Corporation, and now operates as a wholly owned subsidiary of ITT. Since the merger, Rayonier's production has increased to a phenomenal 249,206,000 board feet of lumber, 1,054,000 metric tons of pulp and 43,426,000 square feet of plywood. The annual capacity of lumber from the Hoquiam operations alone is 70,000,000 board feet—not including the other five mills in Washington, New Brunswick, Georgia, South Carolina, and Florida.

Through it all, the railroad played a major role, as it will long into the future. Even with today's modern overland transport trucks, moving the logs out of the woods by rail continues to be the safest, most economical method. □

This photo lends credence to the tales abounding in Carson City of giant timber stands out on the Olympic Peninsula of Washington State. The logs pictured here at the New London unload will soon be dumped from their "disconnects" into the Hoquiam River. (H.G. Nelson photo, Rayonier collection)

Above, a small Howe truss bridge over a log slough in the Hoquiam area, exact location unidentified. (H.G. Nelson photo, Rayonier collection)

Below, Robert Polson, top row, left, poses with his family, dressed in their Sunday finest, in front of the home they lived in prior to the one which later became the Polson museum. (H.G. Nelson photo, Rayonier collection)

Robert Polson, who joined his brother Alex to form the Polson Brothers Logging Company. (H.G. Nelson photo, William D. Jones collection)

One of Polson's original steam donkeys helps lay a skid road leading out of Camp 2. Note the hand saw, or "misery whip" blade resting on a ledge on the donkey. In these days, despite the aid of the steam donkey, logging was hard, backbreaking work, and only the toughest men could perform such labor. (H.G. Nelson photo, Rayonier collection)

A very early wide-face; builder, date and location unknown. This machine helped hoist logs onto waiting rail cars. (H.G. Nelson photo, Rayonier collection)

Above, one of the old Howe truss-type swing spans at Hoquiam in the very early days of railroading in the Grays Harbor area. It was built entirely of wood beams and steel tie rods, and swiveled on rollers in the center. Note the two men perched atop the bridge tower. (H.G. Nelson photo, Rayonier collection)

Below, one of the Dolbeer donkeys at work in the woods. (H.G. Nelson photo, Rayonier collection)

Above, Camp 4 acquires a modern piston-valve "Tacoma" yarder featuring piston valves instead of the slide valves used on earlier donkeys. Note the long saw blade slung over the should of the man on

the ground. Several years would pass before power saws became available. (H.G. Nelson photo, Rayonier collection)

Below, a steam donkey, with its drag-line bucket hooked up, grades a line for a new spur to the timber. (H.G. Nelson photo, Rayonier collection)

17

Above, a newly purchased steam donkey sits on a siding, waiting to be outfitted with spools, water tank, fuel bunker and other assorted items before reporting for duty. Note the idler trucks attached ahead of her as she gets tied into the train. (H.G. Nelson photo, Rayonier collection)

Below, a construction detail takes a break with the Bucyrus-Erie steam shovel while grading for more rail to be laid at Camp 7. The large pin in the lower center of the photo is one of the stabilizers, set at the corners, to keep the shovel from rocking as it moves heavy loads of earth. (H.G. Nelson photo, Rayonier collection)

Above, Polson photographer H.G. Nelson labeled this scene "In the Big Cut" near Camp 7. Note the pile of firewood on the rear deck. The two hand shovels leaning against the steam shovel prove the timelessness of a good, basic design. (H.G. Nelson photo, Rayonier collection)

Below, Ol' Betsy on the main line, so identified by its well-laid square-cut ties supporting a smooth and level track, a sight not seen on the early spurs. (H.G. Nelson photo, Rayonier collection)

Above, in the early years—in an effort to get the road slapped down as quickly as possible—ties and rail were laid directly over the old skid roads, as can be seen under these disconnects. Later the main line was ballasted and upgraded for heavy daily usage by larger lokeys. The spurs never knew such luxury—they were intended to be used only long enough to log the immediate area, then were abandoned or ripped out.

The wood-beam pilot on the Baldwin 4-6-0 was later removed. (H.G. Nelson photo, Rayonier collection)

Below, the wood burning No. 45, left, and an unidentified lokey pose

with rail hands and unidentified company officials or visitors at Camp 7 in the early 1900s. (H.G. Nelson photo, Rayonier collection)

Above, the Northern Pacific used this Ten Wheeler to haul products from the Moclips area to Tacoma, Washington via NP's coastal route. (H.G. Nelson photo, Rayonier collection)

The No. 11 brings a corps of executives out to inspect operations in the woods. (H.G. Nelson photo, Rayonier collection)

Above, this publicity shot of the Polson roster appeared in the local press in the 1940s. The location is believed to be just out of Railroad Camp towards Axford Prairie. (C. Kinsey photo, Rayonier collection)

Below, the sailing ship Alert, *one of many three- and four-masted schooners that plied the Northwest waters in the early days, takes on a load of Polson Brothers timber at the Hoquiam docks. (H.G. Nelson photo, Rayonier collection)*

Below, the little Three-spot works a heavy load of logs through the trackage at Railroad Camp shortly after the Rayonier takeover. This Lima Shay survived the scrapper's torch and is on display near Humptulips. Note the velocipede in the left foreground. (H.G. Nelson photo, William D. Jones collection)

Above, a clean Two-spot gives off a throaty whistle as she crosses a log dump at Moclips just prior to interchanging her cars of logs with the Northern Pacific, which then took them on to a Rayonier

pulp mill at Shelton, Washington. (Stan Kistler photo, Paul Pauly collection)

Below, the No. 111 pulls into the scale yard from Camp 3 late in 1965. (Al Farrow collection)

Above, the 1942 roster lines up at Railroad Camp for a Polson Brothers publicity photo. (C. Kinsey photo, Buster Corrigan collection)

Below, having struck out in his search for gold, Alex Polson struck it rich in lumber and built this handsome home—replete with veranda, upstairs porch, boardwalk and fire hydrant—for his family in Hoquiam, Washington. Although the house has long since been razed, Robert's home, built just to the west, still stands and is the site of today's Polson Museum. (H.G. Nelson photo, Rayonier collection)

Despite World War II, the Polson show continued to haul timber from the Olympic range. Showing off a handsome load are Paul Pauly, second from left, and George Groseclose, second from right, along with two unidentified men. (Dell Mulkey photo, Paul Pauly collection)

For a Christmas card, Rayonier used a photo of the No. 120, superimposed with a winter scene photo. (Bill Evans photo, Buster Corrigan collection)

Chapter Two
The Early Days

In the days before the railroads, felled trees were hauled out of the woods on "skid roads" made from pairs of logs set end-to-end in the ground, forming a makeshift trough. Wet and muddy, the logs formed a slippery base on which to slide or "skid" the felled timber, one log at a time, down to the river, where they were floated to the mill to be cut to final size and shape. The power source was none other than men and oxen. Grit, muscle and sweat moved the logs, a process which was not only tough and dangerous, but painfully slow. Life in the woods was rigorous—more than some, even the toughest, could take. If a bucker or pair of fallers didn't show up, shivering, at the crowded bunkhouse after a day's work, it was presumed they got disgusted and walked off the job. Every now and then, however, a worker would later be discovered pinned by a wayward log or, having slipped from a moss-slick log or rock, lying injured on the ground. Many who might ordinarily have survived an accident bled to death because no one knew they had been injured. Even if someone knew, medical help was so far away that frequently it made no difference.

The oxen, too, were a concern. They required an enormous amount of food and, though by nature a hearty beast, they did occasionally become sick and needed to be cared for. They sometimes became lame; the old ones died and had to be disposed of; young replacements had to be purchased, brought to the site, and broken in. Regardless of how strong they were, they were slow. Granted, they had more brute strength than man, and they could be teamed up to move logs that men could only dream of moving, but the more oxen that were yoked together, the slower the team became. In an industrious nation where growth and progress were the buzzwords of the day, slow was no longer good enough.

Mechanical power set the Industrial Revolution into motion and, once steam came to the forest, logging would never be the same. One of the earliest pieces to turn up in the woods was an invention called the steam donkey. Operating on the same principle as the locomotive, it had a vertical boiler which provided steam for an engine that powered a winch. It was hauled by oxen or rail to a logging site, then fired up so it could drag bucked logs to the skid roads, or later, to waiting rail cars. The donkey's boiler was of a simpler design than that of the horizontal locomotive boiler. A firebox at the base heated a water-filled cylinder directly above, allowing heat to rise naturally through flues placed inside the tank, then out a stack at the top. On a locomotive, steam exhausting mechanically up the stack drew heat artificially through horizontal flues. Because of the donkey's vertical design, water was always over the crown sheet separating the fire box from the water, an advantage when it was positioned on a mountainside. If the boiler of a locomotive sloped too far—as on a steep grade—the water left the crown sheet. The fire's intense heat would quickly burn a hole in the crown sheet, and a catastrophic boiler explosion would instantly scatter the lokey and crew in all directions.

Steam locomotives and steam donkeys worked side by side, and some of the earliest ones were adaptations of each other. Out in the forest you made do with what you had, and if you needed a lokey more than a donkey, you converted the donkey. However, once steam was implemented, specialization was not far behind. Besides donkeys, cranes and a host of auxiliary equipment, soon there were main line locomotives, lokeys for the spurs, and those specializing in steep grades, sharp curves, soft earth, or whatever condition the wood could impose. This is the fascination of logging in the steam era.

(H.G. Nelson photo, Rayonier collection)

The early rail equipment was of course very primitive and dangerous, but it attracted a special breed of man. "In the old days you never had any trouble getting a job," says one old-timer, "since there were so many logging camps around and the need for experienced men was always great. Everyone wanted to work on the railroads then, too, because it was an exciting job and the pay was damn good." The railroad men were in closer contact with each other than other loggers, but it was still dangerous work. Before the advent of air brakes and standards set forth by the Association of American Railroads, handling and making up trains was a perilous task. If someone's hand got caught between link-and-pin couplers, it could be severed without warning. Logs shifting on the bunks were capable of crushing a leg or a whole man. And since early rail was laid without substantial roadbed in soft, muddy terrain, the rails would often sink or spread under the train's weight, causing a derailment. Embankments were known to give way, causing entire trains to plunge, taking their crews with them.

But despite the dangers, the Polson operation was regarded as a good one. Accidents happened, but the injury rate was far lower than for most operations. Paul Pauly, an old trainmaster who was born in 1898 and began working the log trains in 1919 remembers the Rayonier operation well: "We had our share of accidents, all right, but I must say Rayonier had the fewest I ever saw. I guess I got just as bad as anybody when I fell off a log and broke my back. We had our share of derails and dumped logs, but nothing serious as to injury, though. Whenever we had an accident it would of course ball things all up for awhile, until we could get the line cleared, but that was all in a day's work. One time I remember a freak accident that Bobby Rogers had with the 38, coming down with a short train of about 14 cars, I think, when one of the logs slipped and fell off and the big end rolled back up on the rail and locked up under the journal box of the next car and derailed the rest of the train. Then we'd just have to call Bob Hattan out with the crane and pick it all up."

Hattan, a "hostler" and crane operator who worked for Rayonier from 1958 until he retired in 1968, adds, "When I ran the crane there at Rayonier, it never did stop. We used it every day to push cars around, lift loads, move stuff around all day around camp, not to mention the times we were out on the line taking care of problems and routine maintenance. It was much the same as any logging railroad, and we had to go out all the time and pick up derails, dumped logs, or pick up a car through a split switch or any one of a thousand little problems. We couldn't lift the Mallets or diesels, though. They weighed too much, and that took another lokey or a high lead to toll them back on the rail." And old-time Engineer Buster Corrigan remembers: "The Polson road was a good one, and in all my years right up through the Rayonier takeover, until I retired, I never saw a drop of blood. The early days, with the disconnects—we called them 'high trucks'—were the bad times 'cause you had no air on them, only on the engine. These high trucks had to be braked down by hand with a brakeman riding them, and turning the brakes down with a 'hickey,' and this of course took time. He had to anticipate the grade, the load, speed, weight, and all that sort of stuff, and if he didn't get to it on time, you'd have a runaway. One time though—I think in was in 1938—I was firing the No. 70 and we were shoving 25 high trucks about 10 miles above Humptulips, just out of Camp 6 when, without warning, she just upped and heaved over against the bank. The track was soft—you know, it rains here all the time—and everything was mushy. The disconnects had gone through okay, but when the lokey hit the soft spot with her weight she split the rail out of gauge, and went on the ground. We weren't going fast, so no real problems were there, she just started to settle in the dirt. It was a hell of a feeling, though, since she was falling on my side of the loco. When she went, everybody jumped for the weeds, and I couldn't get to the high side, so I just sat her out and rode her down. I was unusual that it happened where it did, 'cause anywhere else she would've rolled all the way over. In all that trackage all up and down the line, this was the only place were we had a close embankment by the tracks, and this is where she chose to go. I often today wonder about that."

A runaway was no laughing matter. One logger tells of a Shay that got away one day and it was the last thing she ever did. Soon going too fast to be shut down, she kept picking up speed until she was hopelessly out of control and abandoned by her crew. The momentum forced the entire gear mechanism to turn so fast that it bent all the rods, spun the pistons faster than the oil could lubricate them, and just "fried" the engine. When the poor lokey finally came to rest after jumping the rails, all that was left was a twisted mass of metal whose only value was quoted in pounds of scrap.

Railroading has come a long was since those days and, while still hard work, it is definitely a safer occupation. "Blowing steam" around the bunkhouse, today's crews all admit it's easier and safer now, compared to the early years. Not as nostalgic, not as awesome, not as adventuresome, but quieter and more efficient. They say you had to handle an old steam lokey like a lady, and if you didn't treat her right, she'd let you know in no uncertain terms. She'd drop her fire, blow her steam, and slip all over the place if you tried to push her. But handle her well, and she'd work her tail off for you. □

A rare photo of one of the early skid roads, also called "pole roads" or "fore-and-aft roads." Logs were "skidded"—one at a time—along the slippery surface. It is interesting to note that the term "skid row," which today refers to a decayed urban area populated by old derelicts, has its origin in the woods. Before portable bunkhouses moved about on rail cars, makeshift shacks for the crews were constructed alongside logging areas, then abandoned when the operation moved on. Later, hobos would take up residence in them. (H.G. Nelson photo, Rayonier collection)

Above, four big wide-face Tacoma yarders pack up and move to higher ground. These donkeys will ride on disconnects to a new logging area, *then be positioned as necessary in the woods. (H.G. Nelson photo, Rayonier collection)* *Below, a very early yarder.*

Below, a Tacoma yarder and its crew at Camp 5. (H.G. Nelson photo, Rayonier collection)

Top, left, known as waddlers, a name earned from the swaying and rocking created by forces imposed on the drive system, the Climaxes had their faults, but they stayed on the rails and were good performers when it came to logging. The two-truck No. 11 shown here was purchased by Polson in 1902, as well as a sister engine in 1903, which was No.12, shown in the artwork below. Both were 50-tonners that Polson sold many years before the Rayonier takeover. However, two larger three-truck Climaxes, purchased as part of the Bloedel Donovan holdings, did operate on the Clallam Branch for a few years under Rayonier ownership. (H.G. Nelson photo, Rayonier collection)

Below, left, wood-burning Climax No. 11 works on filling in the old approach trestle on the high side of the Humptulips bridge approach. Climaxes are easily identified by their canted cylinders. (H.G. Nelson photo, Rayonier collection)

Polson Logging Co.
12

Though not positively identified, these are believed to be the pilings for the first bridge to span the Humptulips River near Camp 7.

Piles were driven, bent by bent, out to the water's edge, then the steel truss was set into place. (H.G. Nelson photo, Rayonier collection)

Above, a family on an outing
pauses for a comfort stop on the
banks of the Humptulips River. The
approach to the bridge in the
background was rebuilt twice after
this photo was taken. (H.G. Nelson
photo, Rayonier collection)

Below, the No. 38 courts trouble—
note the slipped log on the second
bunk. In the foreground are pilings
from a previous trestle on the New
Steven Creek. (Al Farrow
collection)

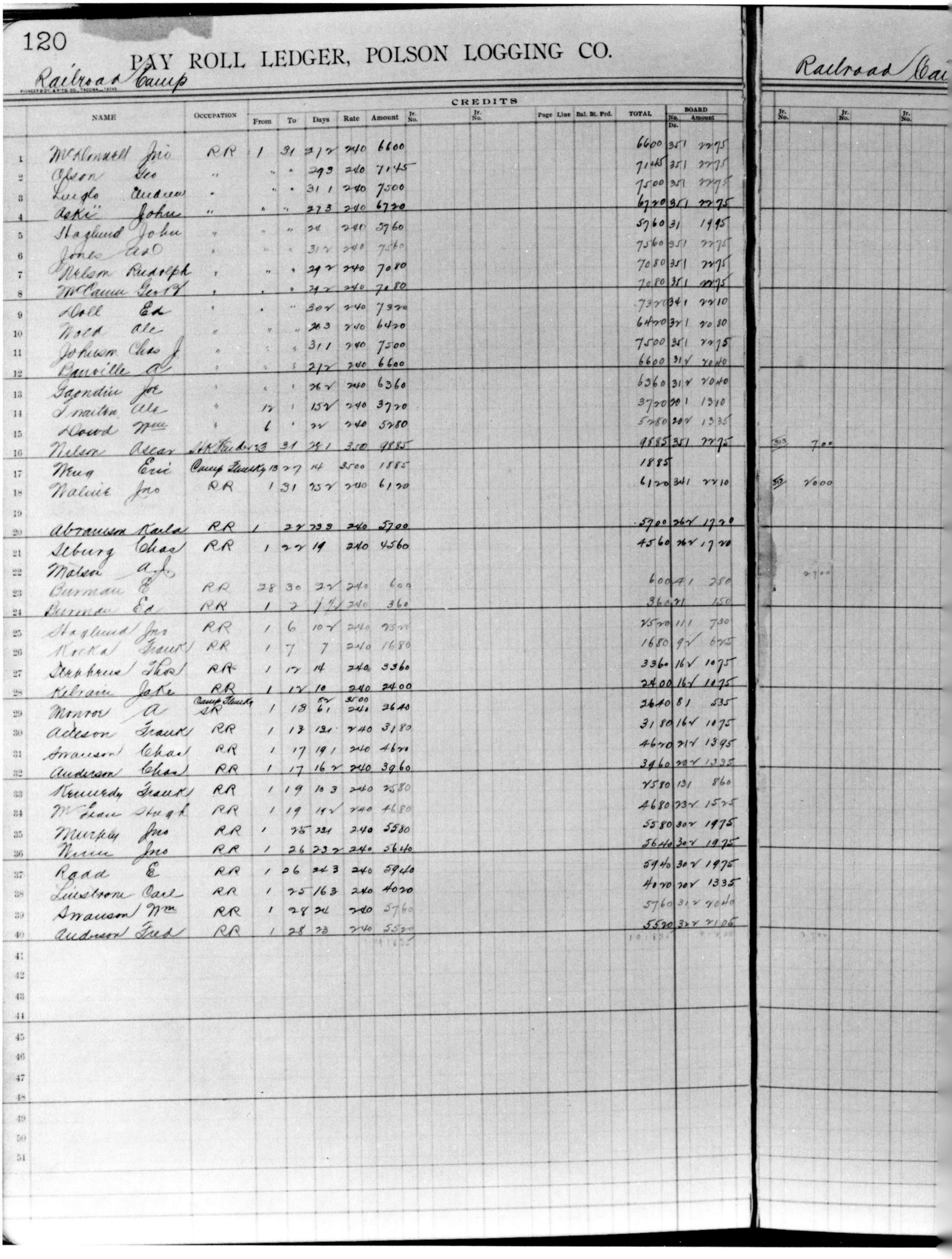

120

PAY ROLL LEDGER, POLSON LOGGING CO.

Railroad Camp

Railroad Ca[illegible]

	NAME		OCCUPATION	CREDITS From	To	Days	Rate	Amount	TOTAL	BOARD No. Ds.	BOARD Amount	Jr. No.	
1	McConnell	Jno	RR	1	31	272	240	6600	6600	351	2275		
2	Olson	Geo	"	"	"	293	240	7145	7145	351	2275		
3	Luglo	Andrew	"	"	"	311	240	7500	7500	351	2275		
4	Aski	John	"	"	"	273	240	6720	6720	351	2275		
5	Haglund	John	"	"	"	24	240	5760	5760	31	1995		
6	Jones	Ed	"	"	"	312	240	7560	7560	351	2275		
7	Nelson	Rudolph	"	"	"	292	240	7080	7080	351	2275		
8	McCann	Geo V	"	"	"	292	240	7080	7080	351	2275		
9	Holl	Ed	"	"	"	302	240	7320	7320	341	2210		
10	Wold	Ole	"	"	"	263	240	6420	6420	321	2080		
11	Johnson	Chas J	"	"	"	311	240	7500	7500	351	2275		
12	Banville	A	"	"	"	272	240	6600	6600	312	2040		
13	Gagndin	Joe	"	"	"	262	240	6360	6360	312	2040		
14	Smalton	Ole	"	12	"	152	240	3720	3720	201	1310		
15	Howard	Wm	"	6	"	22	240	5280	5280	202	1335		
16	Nelson	Oscar	Stk Tender	23	31	281	350	9885	9885	351	2275	313	700
17	Wong	Eric	Camp Flunky	13	27	14	3500	1885	1885				
18	Walnie	Jno	RR	1	31	252	240	6120	6120	341	2210	313	2000
19													
20	Abramson	Karla	RR	1	27	233	240	5700	5700	262	1720		
21	Seburg	Chas	RR	1	22	19	240	4560	4560	262	1720		
22	Malson	A. J.											2700
23	Burman	E	RR	28	30	22	240	600	600	41	280		
24	Burman	Ed	RR	1	2	1½	240	360	360	21	150		
25	Haglund	Jno	RR	1	6	102	240	2520	2520	111	730		
26	Kocka	Frank	RR	1	7	7	240	1680	1680	92	625		
27	Stephens	Thos	RR	1	12	14	240	3360	3360	162	1075		
28	Kelrain	Jake	RR	1	12	10	240	2400	2400	162	1075		
29	Monroe	A	Camp Flunky SR	1	18	52 61	3500 240	2640	2640	81	535		
30	Adeson	Frank	RR	1	13	131	240	3180	3180	162	1075		
31	Swanson	Chas	RR	1	17	191	240	4620	4620	212	1395		
32	Anderson	Chas	RR	1	17	162	240	3960	3960	202	1335		
33	Kennedy	Frank	RR	1	19	103	240	2580	2580	131	860		
34	McLean	Hugh	RR	1	19	192	240	4680	4680	232	1525		
35	Murphy	Jno	RR	1	25	231	240	5580	5580	302	1975		
36	Winn	Jno	RR	1	26	232	240	5640	5640	302	1975		
37	Rodd	E	RR	1	26	243	240	5940	5940	302	1975		
38	Linstrom	Carl	RR	1	25	163	240	4020	4020	202	1335		
39	Swanson	Wm	RR	1	28	24	240	5760	5760	312	2040		
40	Anderson	Fred	RR	1	28	23	240	5520	5520	322	2105		
41													
42													
43													
44													
45													
46													
47													
48													
49													
50													
51													

Hospital	Page	Line	Amt.Brt.Frd.	Total Debits	Bal. Due	Jr.No.	Amt. of Chk.	Date	Chk. No.	Page	Line	BAL. FORD. Cr.	Dr.	
100				27.50	38.50							38.50		1
100				24.55	46.90							46.90		2
100				27.50	47.50							47.50 ✓		3
100				23.75	43.45							43.45		4
100				21.95	35.65							35.65		5
100				23.75	57.85							57.85		6
100				38.10	32.70							32.70 ✓		7
100				38.45	31.85							31.85		8
100				24.35	48.85							48.85		9
100				31.95	32.25							32.25		10
100				27.90	46.10							46.10 ✓		11
100				22.85	43.15							43.15		12
100				23.90	39.70							39.70		13
100				16.35	20.85							20.85		14
100				19.60	33.20							33.20		15
100				43.35	55.50							55.50		16
100				2.00	14.85	515	14.85		761					17
100				57.05	4.15							4.15		18
														19
100				21.20	35.80	30	35.80		275					20
100				22.85	22.75	59	22.75		222					21
														22
				3.45	2.55	29	2.55		17					23
				1.50	2.10	23	2.10		9					24
				7.30	17.90	25	17.90		43					25
				6.25	10.55	24	10.55		81					26
100				20.60	13.00	56	13.00		117					27
				20.25	3.25	30	3.25		118					28
				18.55	7.85	51	7.85		124					29
100				13.00	18.80	308	18.80		142					30
100				22.70	23.50	318	23.50		157					31
100				21.50	18.10	311	18.10		156					32
100				19.15	5.95	311	5.95		200					33
100				23.55	23.25	311	23.25		201					34
100				30.00	25.80	313	25.80		246					35
100				26.90	29.50	312	29.50		255					36
100				22.05	37.35	311	37.35		254					37
				17.00	23.20	312	23.20		257					38
100				30.20	27.40	314	27.40		282					39
100				23.70	31.50	315	31.50		283					40
														41
														42
														43
														44
														45
														46
														47
														48
														49
														50
														51

A January 1905 payroll ledger for Railroad Camp employees. Workers made $2.40 per day, paid their own rent at camp, plus food and miscellaneous items. That didn't leave much at the end of the month, although some proclaimed the pay was "damn good." (H.G. Nelson photo, William D. Jones collection)

Above, loaded with the day's haul of timber, Shay No. 33 prepares to depart for the New London unload, and then on down to Railroad Camp. The brakeman on the ground is identified by the iron bar he holds. Called a hickey, it was used to tie down the brakes on rail cars as the "brakie" ran alongside.

This Shay was a typical "steam jammer," equipped only with a primitive steam brake. Note the unusual maintenance-of-way cars behind the lokey. (H.G. Nelson photo, Rayonier collection)

Below, loggers pose atop a seven-foot-diameter log, representing

10,000 board feet of lumber. The log rests on a pair of very early wooden log bunks built back in the 1800s. These cars had no couplers; their wagon tongues and pins were tied together with heavy rope. Lacking springs and brakes, they were very tricky to handle. (H.G. Nelson photo, Rayonier collection)

Above, in the early days of logging by rail, timber was loaded onto disconnects, held in place by large wooden chocks, wrapped with a chain, and moved on out. Note the severely worn flanges on the "high trucks" in the foreground. (H.G. Nelson photo, Rayonier collection)

Below, a pair of Dewitt disconnect log bunks in the car shops at Railroad Camp in the early 1900s. These were built from strap iron and wood beams and were considered very modern for their time, since they were equipped with brakes, although the brakes still *had to be tied down by hand. (H.G. Nelson photo, Rayonier collection)*

This accident occurred in 1938 while the No. 70 was pushing twenty-five sets of high trucks up a hill just past Camp 6. Heavy rains had softened the roadbed and the rails spread under the lokey's weight. This was the only point along the line where there was an embankment alongside the track to cushion the fall, and the engine happened to land softly against a stump, which prevented her from going clear over on her side. Buster Corrigan was not able to jump out of the cab, so all he could do was hang on. He came through it without a scratch. (Buster Corrigan collection)

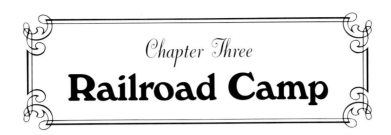

Chapter Three

Railroad Camp

Railroad Camp was where all the action was during the heyday of steam. As far back as 1902 the Polson Brothers began laying track from the New London log dump to a point approximately seven miles up the line. This point became Railroad Camp. The main shops were located here, along with storage yards, supplies, sidings for extra rail equipment, train wreck equipment, the "bone yard," and all the necessary items needed to support the railroad. Here also was the superintendent's office, as well as the main dispatcher's office and bunkhouses for the crews. Hustle and bustle was constant. Clanking and banging of steel and iron was heard daily in the shops as mechanics, boilermen, and blacksmiths repaired or rebuilt whatever was necessary to maintain smooth operation on the rails.

These men were a proud lot. They maintained their equipment, cars and lokeys like a Class I mainline railroad. The Railroad Camp crews often boasted that they could build you a lokey right here in camp from barstock, boiler plate, and whatever parts were laying around. They didn't have to rely on the outside for repairs, either. As equipment was purchased, often as used items from other logging shows, it was brought into camp and the car rebuilder would overhaul the trucks and brake rigging, and even replace the whole center beam if necessary. In the early years the lokeys were kept in tip-top shape, wiped down clean every day, inspected and repaired as necessary. Operation was under the jurisdiction of the Northwest timber division, headquartered down at Hoquiam, which also had the engineering department, the industrial relations department, and the planning and programming force. Over the years as the main line moved further and further up into the woods, the loggers began to move their bunkhouses out of Railroad Camp and on to other camps, but the rail operations continued to be based here, maintaining the central spot clear up to the end of the steam era.

During the peak of operations trains ran daily, bringing the timber down to the New London unloading docks a short distance form Hoquiam. A day at Railroad Camp began in the wee hours. Long before sunrise, cars were lined up for the 43-mile trip to the camps out of Grays Harbor; the skeletons had to be up in the woods early in the day to load the thousands of board feet of timber for the day's run back down to the mill.

The Grays Harbor main line traverses U.S. Highway 101 for several miles, weaving in and out of the timber, and crosses the highway approximately four miles from Railroad Camp near Humptulips at Axford Prairie. At the height of the activity there was also a line northeast out of Railroad Camp to Camp 3, but the primary line continued up to Camp 14 near Lake Quinalt, and then on to the terminus at Crane Creek. All the spurs split off into the woods from this line.

At the time the Polson Brothers first established Railroad Camp, they used disconnects and the venerable little switcher "Ol' Betsy." There remains considerable controversy over this locomotive. According to past and present Rayonier lore she lived her entire life as Ol' Betsy—named after a sister of the Polsons. But she apparently was the first steam locomotive owned by the Northern Pacific Railway, who had given her the Indian name "Minnetonka," then sold her to Polson during World War I. The NP later wanted her back, to put on display as an historical exhibit, but she was a valuable locomotive to Polson—who was too busy hauling timber to be very concerned about history—and he was not eager to sell her. After much negotiation the Northern Pacific managed to secure her from Polson in 1933, but not without giving up in trade a much larger 2-8-0 Consolidation. Burlington Northern later bought out the Northern Pacific but still has the cherished switcher on display as the Minnetonka. The Consolidation taken in trade—worth three times the price of Ol' Betsy—was the NP's No. 51, built in 1889, and used by Rayonier until scrapped in 1948.

As the years went by, the Polson Brothers continued to lay rail into the woods, acquiring more rolling stock and bigger lokeys to handle the increased haul. In 1905 they purchased a 65-ton Consolidation, and shortly after, a 45-ton 2-6-0 Mogul to handle the loads down the main line to New London. Later a couple of old 4-6-0 Ten Wheelers were added to the roster, as well as more Shays and Climaxes, whose gear-driven wheels gave effective power at low speeds. They were also sprung to handle steep grades and uneven rail, where the drivers of a rigid-frame rod engine would slip. One of the Ten Wheelers was the No. 10, which Alex McClean "Mac" Polson, Alex's nephew, fired frequently. "The Ten-Spot was a good steamer," he said, "and all the controls were handy and easy to work. I don't recall how old she was, but one of the drivers had a scrap stamp on it dated 1863. Now, I don't know if it had been put on the engine during repair work, or if it was the original, but that lokey was old, I can tell you that. Later, after we bought some heavier lokeys, we used the old Ten-spot for laying rail, and in those days we'd lay a half mile a day with a crew of 20 to 25 men. In those days that was a lot of rail with a small crew, but we had perfected a pretty fast method. Two men would lay the ties on the grade, after being dumped off the flats. Then some men would hoist the rail on top of the ties, and two men would lay the bridles between the rail and we'd run the Ten-spot on up the new track while the spikers would come up behind the engine and spike the track, pull the bridles and move them up ahead of the engine. It was a pretty easy job for the 'tallowpot' 'cause we weren't working the engine, so he really had little to do, just keep a spot fire in her boiler and relax. This didn't set too well, though, with the steel gang boss, old Mickey 'the Rat' Lawlus, they called him—a small feisty-as-hell Irishman—so he'd yell up to the cab and make the fireman get down and help the track gang."

As the Grays Harbor main line was being pushed further and further toward Crane Creek in the late 1930s, the Polson show realized the need for a larger engine. They negotiated with the Northern Pacific for one of their 2-6-6-2 compound Mallets—with two independent sets of drivers under a common boiler, for more flexibility on curves—and succeeded in acquiring the No. 3100, which had been working the

pass out of Wallace Branch. It was one of six the Baldwin Locomotive Works built for the Northern Pacific as the road's class Z-1. Polson bought the lokey for a mere $11,436.37 in cash and put her right to work. It didn't take long for the NP to regret its decision to sell. The company soon came back to Polson and offered up to $85,000 for her. The NP needed her badly, but so did Polson and, as with Ol' Betsy, the answer was "no." This time Polson didn't budge. The deal never was completed and No. 3100 worked for Polson and then Rayonier until, old and decrepit, she succumbed to the scrapper's torch in 1959. The 3100, though a hard-working locomotive, was troublesome. She was heavy, hard on track—"that blunderbuss just rolled the rail over all the time"—and dirty, but according to hostler Bob Hattan, "they worked that poor old lokey to her grave. She'd take off in the morning up the line out of Railroad Camp, and you couldn't even see her for all the steam leaks and smoke. She leaked everywhere, and blew slobber all over the place, and was just a filthy mess all the time, but she did work, and gave a day's work for a day's pay. They repacked her and tightened her up and did everything they could, but she just kept on blowing and gunking up everything." Buster Corrigan was the engineer who ran her most of the time and described the 3100 as "a saturated steam blunderbuss, and real hard on track, so you had to handle her carefully. Over the years she began cracking her frames all the time and you had to inspect her before each run. If cracks did develop, you had to nurse her down light to the shops and get 'em welded before the next run. She did her job, though, even with all the problems she had. Hell, during the war we needed her so badly just to get the timber out, we couldn't afford to sell her back to the NP or locate any other power to replace her. She had her problems, but if you were careful with her, you could get the job done."

When Rayonier bought out the Polsons in 1948 it continued to add to the roster. In 1945, prior to the Polson purchase, Rayonier had bought the Bloedel Donovan holdings up in the northern section of the Olympic peninsula and began what was called the Clallam Branch operation at that site. This line, built by Bloedel Donovan in the '30s, was actually surveyed by the Milwaukee Road many years before, but was never utilized by that company. The expanding Clallam operation significantly increased the need for more equipment and motive power, so once again Rayonier went shopping. This time it sought more Mallets, as well as Mikados and smaller lokeys to handle the spurs. Besides locomotives, the roster by now boasted some 600 skeleton cars of various shapes and sizes, and a large collection of maintenance equipment. By then World War II was in full swing, creating shortages, despite the fact that the equipment was urgently needed, so everything had to be purchased used, surplus, or by whatever means possible. Rayonier had at this time hundreds of miles of track laid throughout the forest, and to keep the operation going it relied on a legion of Mallets, Mikados, Prairies, Moguls, Shays, Climaxes, and Heislers. During this time Rayonier did manage to order 125 new log bunks from American Car & Foundry, but everything else on the property was scared up any way possible.

The Clallam operation was not as grand a show as the Grays Harbor line, but it presented a distinct challenge to the logistics of railroading. Winding through treacherous curves and dizzying heights, this line ran out of Sekiu on the Strait of Juan de Fuca, southward to Hoko, and on through Dickey Camp to the end of the line near Forks. There was also a secondary line to Beaver and Sappho, with its attendant spurs penetrating the logging areas. By 1957 the rugged Clallam Branch had played out and Rayonier started closing it down. Track was ripped up and sold for scrap, lokeys were cut to pieces, and the vast timberlands were returned to Mother Nature. Because of the contemptuous terrain the Clallam spurs required Shays and Climaxes, while three old 2-6-6-2 Mallets, retained from Bloedel Donovan, worked the Clallam main line to the log dump. Engines No. 8 and 9 were sidetank Mallets, while No. 14 was a Mallet with tender, a sister to 38 and 120 on the Grays Harbor line. After years up on the Clallam line No. 14 was floated by barge—there was no direct rail connection—to Grays Harbor, where she worked the main line out of Railroad Camp until ultimately cut up for scrap. Thanks to a devoted railfan, the Eight-spot survived the torch and, though not in the best shape, is still capable of firing up and doing what she was built to do.

Out on the Clallam Branch where timber was unusually high and grades uncommonly steep, some logging areas were rendered inaccessible by rail. Loggers then attached cables to spar trees—some as high as 200 feet—and yarded the logs down by steel cable, block and tackle, and steam donkeys pulling, sliding and dragging the timber out after it was cut. Seeing those "sticks" yarded out was not only an awesome sight, but a tribute to logging ingenuity. High lead lines were wrapped around the spar trees and drag lines attached to pulleys and to the donkey drums. The "donkey puncher" had the chore of yarding in the logs after they were choked and the "whistle punk," usually a young lad breaking into the logging game, would whistle signals to the puncher and the rest of the crew. All these men had to know the signals for the movement of the various lines, since in many cases the donkey puncher couldn't see the crews. As the timber was brought down to the landing, it was stacked into decks and then hoisted onto the skeleton cars.

In later years, large yarders and skidders were developed by various manufacturers, such as the Willamette Iron & Steel Company. These iron behemoths had their own high towers, steam donkeys and drums all built on one large frame, and were capable of traversing the rails on their own wheels or aboard log cars. It was dangerous at these loading and yarding sites. Each man jack had to know his position, coordinate almost automatically, and pay attention to his role in the overall show, lest he get caught in what could be a fatal accident. The donkey was usually brought to the logging site on a flat car or skeleton. Then the loggers would run a line out to a tree, couple up the line and the donkey could then pull itself up the location where needed. The spar trees would then be limbed and topped, a sky line secured between two trees, and the rest of the lines attached. These lines could run hundreds of feet up into the cutting areas for yarding logs down to the railhead. After a few weeks, when the area was logged out and it became impractical to continue moving the whole show over brush and timber, the lines would be brought down, the donkeys pulled back down to the railhead, loaded onto railroad cars, and transported to the next new location.

The lokeys did more than just haul logs to the mill—they also performed yeoman duties at the loading sites. If it was impractical to haul a steam donkey up a mountainside or down a steep canyon, the lines were hooked up to a lokey, and she worked her way up and down the rails pulling logs off the makeshift spar trees located near the tracks.

A hundred years ago, as the steam age came into being, the loggers devised the high lead system with steam donkeys that pulled the logs down out of the woods, and the mechanical age had begun. With improvements such as the Dolbeer steam donkeys and later Willamette skidders, the ultimate efficiency of the day was reached, and this type of logging practice has lasted up through the present. Now the roar of diesel engines has replaced the sounds of steam, but the concept is still the same.

The line going up to Camp 3 presented some formidable grades—some as steep as 7%. Geared Shays No. 91 and 191 brought the loads down from Camp 3 to the "make up" where Mikados 2, 70, 90 and 101 took them on down to New London. Later, the "Mikes" were retired and Mallets 110 and 11 took over the line until its closure. Camp 3 eventually played out—after 57 years of operation—and the last log train chugged out in May of 1967. But even as camp was folded, it was the venerable old No. 110 that pulled up the last spar tree and brought down the final load of equipment. "Just before I retired," says Bob Hattan, "I went up to the Camp 3 line and pulled it out with the 110 and brought all the goods down from there. We had such equipment in the early years as Nelson horizontal spool loaders, Willamette loaders and Washington skidders up in the woods, and what we didn't leave, were brought down for use at other locations or scrapped. There was one old Nelson spool loader that was at Humptulips that they couldn't get through the bridge and as far as I know it's still up there today. The Camp 3 line, that was the last one to come out. I went up there with my crews on the 110 and pulled out everything but the rail. Rayonier then sold the track to a scrap dealer, and he came in with a little gas donkey and pulled the rail out and sold it to someone else."

Back down on the Grays Harbor line logging was still the order of the day. Mallet No. 120 was taking her turn on the main line with her sister, No. 14—transferred to Railroad Camp upon the arrival of diesels on the Clallam Branch—as well as the 110 and 111, and No. 38. Also working the line were Mikados 70, 90, 99 and the Two-spot. One of Rayonier's best known locomotives was the 2-6-6-2 "Sierra" No. 38 Compound Mallet. This lokey started out in life as Weyerhaeuser's No. 4, then was sold to the Sierra Railroad in California where her number was changed to 38. While in Sierra's hands she appeared in many movies, and Pacific Fast Mail later issued a brass replica of the locomotive, calling it the "Sierra type." When Rayonier acquired her in 1955 she retained her famous No. 38 and worked the Grays Harbor main line until retiring in the '60s. This lokey was one of the lucky survivors of the torch, and is now on display at Crane Creek. Buster Corrigan,

who "ran all those lokeys for Polson and Rayonier right up to the end and I wouldn't have given anything in trade for it," remembers well the Sierra: "The 38 was a good engine, but she had a hell of a touchy boiler on her and was hard to fire. Some of the firemen wouldn't even get on her, since she was so tricky with water. You'd have a glass full of water one minute, and none the next. Then if you turned the injectors on and filled her with cold water you'd lose all your steam, and that meant building the fire up again, and well, it was just one battle after another to keep her going. Once you got the hang of her, though, and could stay ahead of her, she performed well. It was a lot harder on the fireman than it was for me, 'cause all I had to do was pull the throttle and let the fireman worry about his problems. The No. 14 and the 120 were sister engines to the 38, too, but they didn't seem to have the problems she had."

No. 110 and 111 were tank Mallets. The 2-6-6-2T engines were purchased from Weyerhaeuser without tenders, which Rayonier added later. To hostler Bob Hattan, who had spent many an hour scrubbing old No. 3100, these lokeys' cleanliness was next to Godliness: "The later superheated engines like the 110 and 111 were no problem because they didn't blow like the older lokeys did." The 111 was eventually bought by the California Western Railroad in Fort Bragg where she became—with modifications—Cal Western's No. 46.

The major transfer of loads from the disconnects and skeletons to the log cars was done at Crane Creek. The small tank Mallets brought the loads from the spurs down to the 60-car-long siding at Crane Creek, where they were then reloaded onto bigger log trains for the run to New London. Here the bigger Mallets—No. 14, the Sierra, and No. 120 did their "stack talk" back down the main line toward civilization. At New London the logs were dumped into the river to be rafted on down to Hoquiam.

As time went on, methods became more refined. A big technological leap forward was the switch from telephones to two-way radios. Paul Pauly became Rayonier's trainmaster in 1944 after a slipped disc in his back prevented his working the trains any longer. He remembers, "When I began dispatching after my accident, we used telephones to direct the traffic up and down the line and had as many as 14 trains running in the early days, and it was quite a chore to keep everything going smoothly. I used a track board with the lines drawn on it and would place pins in all the locations where the trains were, and move them as necessary by telephone to the crews, and they had to stop and call me all along the line for clearances. Later, when we got radios, it was a lot easier and shortened the time of the runs a good deal.

The Coming of the Diesels

Through the 1950s the subject of diesels was tossed around Rayonier's boardroom and the usual corps of salesman journeyed out from town to extol the virtues of the "growlers." Although diesels eventually dominated Rayonier's operations, the new-fangled engines didn't immediately chase steam out of the woods. The diesel lokeys were considerably heavier than their steam predecessors and their axle load required heavier rail and more substantial road-bed—a change that wouldn't take place overnight. Mac Polson remembers, "We used untreated ties cut from cedar in the old days, which was okay for the Shays and light rod engines, up until Rayonier came on the property and brought their big Mallets in. We had the 3100, though, and when she hit those old soft cedar sticks, all hell broke loose. She was so heavy and spread out, she tore those ties to pieces in no time. That's when we had to start re-laying creosoted ties, to handle the heavier engines. Rayonier, of course, put new ties in on all the main lines and better ballasting to accommodate the big power on the road." "When we got the diesels, " Bob Hattan adds, "they had to lay new 100-lb. rail for them, 'cause they'd just rip out all the light rail that was there before. Hell, even the 3100 and the 120 and 14 were too big for the light 55- and 60-lb. rail they ran on." The steam lokeys, besides being in excellent shape, were also more proficient at handling the twisting lines into the woods. But when the going got really tough, the job was given to modern diesel transport trucks—it was easier and cheaper to clear a road for an overland truck than to clear a road and lay roadbed and rail for a heavier, more restricted locomotive. On into the late '50s steam was still the backbone of the Rayonier show, though two Baldwin diesels did show up on the property. Still operating out of Railroad Camp were Mallets No. 14, 38,120,110,111 and Mikados No. 70, 90 and the Two-spot. Old and worn, the No. 8 Mallet was still doing her chores up at Sekiu, but everyone knew she was living on borrowed time. The retirement of steam was finally scheduled for 1962-1963,

and Rayonier even held an "End-of-an-Era" ceremony on March 31, 1962. On that day No. 90 and the famed Sierra hauled the symbolic "last log train pulled by steam," thereby turning over the line to the modern diesels. But the guillotine didn't actually fall until 1967. Though the major portion of Rayonier's steam roster was retired to the "boneyard" at Railroad Camp, lokeys 38, 110, and 11 were kept on standby to fire up when the diesels wouldn't.

Old locomotives somehow refuse to die. No. 111 of course, went to the California Western Railroad. Sans tanks and sporting a new square-box tender built over her original slopeback, she ran excursions as the "Super Skunk." The Two-spot was sold to several operators in the Mideastern states some time ago. Shay No. 3, another survivor, is now on display at Promised Land Park near Humptulips. After retiring from Rayonier, No. 70, a beautiful little Mikado, ran for several years at the Puget Sound Railroad and Historical Society in Snoqualmie Falls until 1974, when a crack in her backhead shut her down. She is still on the property, with plans to repair her and run her again. The 45 has been preserved and is on display in downtown Hoquiam, and No. 90 is on display at Garibaldi, Oregon, with hopes of making her once again able to perform. And the Sierra? She may also ride the rails in years to come. Though never a strong lokey and plagued with leaks even in her prime, there is talk of taking her to a local museum and fixing her up. But the old gray mare will need a lot of attention. One "hogger" said that her poor old frame had been welded so much that she had no frame—just one solid weld from her rear drivers to the front set. The driver springs are all flat and the brass all gone, but aside from those "small details," yes she could run again.

Now there's nothing left of Railroad Camp except weeds and brush, but the memories linger as you stand where the old enginehouse stood for so many years. The memorable aroma of Bunker C oil seems to waft through the air and for a fleeting moment you could swear you fell the throb of a panting locomotive. But a quick blink of the eyes brings you around. Railroad Camp has slipped into history, and all the diesels in the world will never bring it back. □

51

52

Above, an early view of the machine shop at Railroad Camp. Note the belt drives, the steam pipe running across the room at an angle, and the old belt-driven drill press on the left. The workbench was no doubt placed near *many windows because daylight was the shop's primary light source. (H.G. Nelson photo, Rayonier collection)* *Below, Chief Superintendent Bennet Ellingston surveys Railroad Camp on a wet morning. It was his job to see that all rail operations ran smoothly under any circumstances. (H.G. Nelson photo, William D. Jones collection)*

Above, an early view of Railroad Camp while still under contruction. Note the incomplete train sheds, the stack of ties next to the men, the bunkhouse, and the tarp slung over the locomotive at rear, center. The young man

sitting on Shay No. 33 probably grew up to be a crew member or a logger himself. Note the drag bucket in the foreground, next to the stack of ties. (H.G. Nelson photo, Rayonier collection)

Below, shop crews said they could build a lokey right in camp with whatever parts were lying around, and this Skagit gas speeder, used as the Sekiu shop switcher, is testimony to their claim. (Ken Schmelzer collection)

Above, fire equipment car No. 1 was in use though the mid-1960s. Note the solid bunk archbars with no springs. (Ken Schmelzer collection)

Below, fire equipment car No. 2 had an added wooden foot board bolted to the truck. (Ken Schmelzer collection)

Above, this four-wheeled, self-powered car, called a speeder, was built at Railroad Camp. It was used to transport crews and offered cover from the rain. On the front is the box used for guiding the alignment of link-and-pin couplers. (Ken Schmelzer collection)

Below, this unusual maintenance-of-way car was built by Rayonier for use as a wreck-chasing car, containing a welder and air compressor, or anything else needed for emergency track repairs. (Ken Schmelzer collection)

Above, this unusual shingle-sided camp car was used to house the women "flunkies" who worked in the cookhouse. Most had plain horizontal or vertical siding, as on the one *at the left of this photo. The planks on the ground remind us that mud was a fact of life in camp. After a day's work, the women were probably too tired to be bothered by* *the sound the rain made on the corrugated metal roof. (Ken Schmelzer collection)*

Above, this shower car, whose roof is swayback with age, utilizes a sliding door from an old box car. (Ken Schmelzer collection)

Above, shortly after the Polson Brothers Logging Company came into existence, Ol' Betsy, its first locomotive, was at work. Here, with the aid of a rugged crew and the steam donkey in the background, she makes up a short train. In the background at left are more disconnects awaiting their burden. (H.G. Nelson photo, Rayonier collection)

Below, the No. 14 rests her Walschaerts at Camp 14 prior to a day's run. The bunkhouses on the left were probably originally at Railroad Camp, then relocated later. (Al Farrow collection)

Above, the famous "Minnetonka" just prior to her return to the NP, to be put on display in Chicago. The Polson brothers bought her from the NP and named her "Ol' Betsy." The NP later wanted her back so badly that they gave in *trade a locomotive worth three times as much! (H.G. Nelson photo, William D. Jones collection)*

Below, loggers worked the year 'round, and being cold was a fact of life in the woods. Here, Shay No. 55, *purchased in 1907, sits on a siding in the first snow of the season. The lokey was scrapped at Railroad Camp in 1948, the year that the Polson Brothers Logging Company became Rayonier, Inc. (H.G. Nelson photo, Rayonier collection)*

A proud crew poses in front of No. 33, a three-truck Shay purchased by the Polsons in 1905 and scrapped at Railroad Camp in 1947. Note the huge stack of wood in the bunker and the "idler" flat between the engine and the first disconnect. The idler is a safety device. It serves as a spacer between the locomotive and the logs, in case the logs break loose and slide forward. (H.G. Nelson photo, Rayonier collection)

Above, detail of the geared mechanism of a Shay locomotive, an invaluable asset to logging operations of the day. Geared engines, such as the No. 3 shown here, provided more effective power at low speeds and on hills, and they were sprung to absorb the inconsistencies of uneven rail, a

frequent problem encountered in forest terrain. (H.G. Nelson photo, Rayonier collection)

Below, the No. 10, a Baldwin Ten Wheeler, brings a load down from Camp 7. This lokey was purchased from the Union Pacific and was

one of the oldest owned by the Polson Brothers—one of her drivers had a stamp dated 1863 on it, but it's not known whether that was an original or replacement part. She was scrapped at Railroad Camp in 1955. (H.G. Nelson photo, Rayonier collection)

Above, at the New London log dump, the Ten-spot waits for logs to be emptied from the first log car. After the first load of logs was dumped, the lokey would inch forward until the second car was above the water. The process was repeated until every stick was dumped. Equipped only with a "peavey"—a long pole with a hook on the end—these men are unloading the hard way, without the benefit of a crane. (H.G. Nelson photo, Rayonier collection)

Below, the Ten-spot works the Big Cut up near Camp 7. (H.G. Nelson photo, Rayonier collection)

After a route is surveyed and graded with a drag bucket, the "gandy dancers" lay the ties. Next comes the rail—laid, spiked and gauged piece by piece. In later *years a bridle system was developed which greatly increased the amount of rail laid per day. (Both: H.G. Nelson photo, Rayonier collection)*

Above, the cable is taut as the steam jammer takes up the slack on another load of earth being moved to make way for rail at Camp 7. (H.G. Nelson photo, Rayonier collection)

Below, after this log beam trestle near Camp 7 was hastily built across low ground, it was reinforeced with dirt and gravel. This was much quicker and easier than the tedious task of grading and filling with mule or oxen teams and drag buckets. (H.G. Nelson photo, Rayonier collection)

Above, left, the standard four-wheel ballast car was designed to tilt onto the diagonal runners underneath. The sides of the bed were hinged near the top so gravel could spill out. This type of rail car was originally used by railroad contractors for building grades, but *found an equally valuable application in the woods. (Ken Schmelzer collection)*

Above, right, this homemade ballast car, built in the Rayonier shops, came complete with a wooden footboard on the truck *and hand rails for crew members riding on the outside of the car. (Ken Schmelzer collection)*

Below, right, this Pacific Car & Foundry Company maintenance car has long stirrups and arch bar trucks. (Ken Schmelzer collection)

Above, disconnects made by Pacific Car & Foundry, here carrying rail instead of their usual cargo of timber, were the mainstay of the Polson log trains from the very earliest days through the early 1920s. Some-

times called high trucks, each set was independent. A "car" was formed by laying a span of logs over two sets. The rail tongue under the load connecting the trucks was known as a rooster. (Ken Schmelzer collection)

Below, the unusual steel beam trucks of this heavy, all-steel skidder car, manufactured by Pacific Car & Foundry of Seattle, was equipped with swivel trucks to turn the car around by running each truck down separate tracks at a turnout. (Ken Schmelzer collection)

Above, No. 3100, a saturated steam Baldwin, purchased from the Northern Pacific Railroad. The NP later wanted her back and offered over seven times what Polson had paid, but Polson needed her badly and she stayed on the Grays Harbor main line till her dying days. (H.G. Nelson photo, William D. Jones collection)

Below, condemned to death by the cutting torch, the 3100 sits on the "rip track," Railroad Camp's "death row." Note the added sand dome and missing headlight. The 3100 was a hard-working lokey, but was unusually cumbersome. (Ken Schmelzer collection)

Polson Logging Co.
No 3100

James Spencer
76

13'10"

10'6"

3'4"

3'   5'6"   9'6"   5½x10   4'6"
ARCH BAR TRUCKS
15'

27'5½"

3100

PLC   71

15'6"

18'6"

14'6"

20x30   31x30

9'10"   9'2"   9'10"   6'3"   6'6"

28'11"

43'9"

53'8⅝"

VALVE GEAR WALSCHAERT   LOADED WEIGHTS   TRACTIVE POWER 58100
DRIVER DIAMETER 55"   DRIVERS FRONT 126950
BOGIES   30½"   DRIVERS BACK 135400
                             EN.G. TRUCK 21500
                             TRAILER TRUCK 21300
                             TOTAL ENGINE 305150

DRAWN J. SPENCER 1979
FROM ORIGINAL N.P. PRINTS 1935

71

Above, the Two-spot at Railroad Camp, alongside the Sierra's tender, in September 1957. This Mikado was owned by the Saginaw Lumber Company and the Northwest Lumber Company before arriving at the Polson show, and later changed hands three more times. Buster Corrigan had run this lokey when she was at Saginaw, but at Rayonier he ran her sister, the No. 101. (Al Farrow collection)

At right, a clean Two-spot basks in the morning sun at Railroad Camp in the early 1960s. (John Larison photo, Buster Corrigan collection)

Upper right, Willamette No. 2 up on the Sekiu line of the Clallam Branch operation. (Ken Schmelzer collection)

At far right, the No. 2 Willamette gets her flues cleaned out as she goes through routine maintenance at Sekiu in 1956. Note that the gear mechanism is only visible on the right side of the locomotive. The wooden boom on the crane next to her is undoubtedly homemade. Part of Puget Sound, the world's largest inland waterway, is in the background. (Ken Schmelzer collection)

Above, stripped of her headlight and number, this Climax is not easily identified, but is no doubt Polson's No. 12 at Grays Harbor. (H.G. Nelson photo, Rayonier collection)

Below, with rods flapping, the old Eight-spot heads for the woods out of Sekiu with a homemade "crummy" and a string of empties in 1962. By this time she was old and worn, but still working. This lokey is currently stored near Shelton, Washington, awaiting overhaul. (Al Farrow collection)

RAYONIER #9

Above, the Nine-spot, sister to the No. 8 at Dickey Camp. This was one of the lokeys retained from the Bloedel-Donovan show when Rayonier bought it in 1945. (Al Farrow collection)

Above, No. 14 at Sekiu on the Clallam Branch before she was transferred to Railroad Camp. Note the spark arrester on her stack—later replaced with the barrel-type at Railroad Camp. (Al Farrow collection)

Below, Mallet No. 14 prepares for a day's work at Sekiu. When diesels arrived on the Clallam Branch, she was transferred down to Railroad Camp, given another air pump on her side, and

returned to duty on the main line along with her sisters, No. 120 and 38. (Ken Schmelzer collection)

RAYONIER NO. 14
RAILROAD CAMP WASH.

James Spencer
'76

Above, No. 14 at the Sekiu log pond in the 1950s. By this time, steam was on borrowed time, as conversion to diesel power came closer and closer to reality. (Al Farrow collection)

Left, preparing an overloaded skeleton for the trip to New London. Note the steel I-beam bunk in the foreground, the steam donkey in the background, and the array of cables and pulleys to the left. (H.G. Nelson photo, Rayonier collection)

Above, early Dewitt log bunks before a run down from Crane Creek. Note the chocks are nothing more than chunks of wood wedged under the logs. (H.G. Nelson photo, Rayonier collection)

Above, the 191's pilot beam has been cut away along the top edge to make room for the smokebox front when it's removed for maintenance. (William D. Jones photo)

Below, Mikado No. 70, built by Baldwin, in front of the enginehouse at Railroad Camp. (H.G. Nelson photo, William D. Jones collection)

Above, with "Peggy" Roberts and
Buster Corrigan at the helm, the No.
70 brings a small work train up the
hill through old Camp 7 from the
Quinalt River. (Al Farrow collection)

Below, Buster Corrigan and Fireman
Burt Fenton on the No. 90 at the
Humptulips yard, just in from the
woods with a load of timber. (Buster
Corrigan collection)

Above, No. 90 crosses the newly constructed Prairie River bridge in 1961. Note the old trestle's shadow in the creek bed. (Al Farrow collection)

Below, with an array of maintenance equipment tied to her drawbar, the No. 90 crosses the Humptulips River on her way to the woods in July 1957. (Al

Farrow collection)

Above, Mallet No. 111 coming home from a day at Camp 3 with a load of sticks for the mill. (Al Farrow collection)

Below, the 111 handles some switching duties at Camp 3 in June of 1962. At left is another of Rayonier's myriad work cars, this one equipped with heavy foot bars

on the trucks. This lokey would soon be making the journey to Fort Bragg, California to service the California Western Railroad. (Al Farrow collection)

*The No. 101, a 2-8-2 Mikado,
pauses en route to the log dump,
perhaps waiting for clearance to
continue. Note that at the time this
photo was taken, the pilot had been
removed. This lokey, as well as
"Mikes" No. 2, 70 and 90, worked
out of Camp 3 until the more
modern Mallets No. 110 and 111
took over. (H.G. Nelson photo,
Rayonier collection)*

No. 33 and 55, both wood-burning "sidewinders," with their crews at Camp 3 in the early 1900s. The No. 33 has no balloon stack to arrest the sparks and cinders. The shotgun stack, which must have raised havoc with the crews and surrounding woods, was very likely only a temporary measure. (H.G. Nelson photo, Rayonier collection)

Left, No. 110 brings the last load of equipment down from Camp 3 in May 1967. The Camp played out after 57 years of operation. (Pete Replinger photo, Ken Schmelzer collection)

Above, a bird's-eye view of No. 111 switching the Camp 3 transfer in an earlier scene. (Buster Corrigan collection)

Above, the 111, running this trip in reverse, slips and slides downgrade from Camp 3, with flats in tow, in June of 1965. (Al Farrow collection)

Below, shown here in repose before a day's run at Crane Creek, the 111 was originally owned by Weyerhaeuser. It was purchased

without a tender, which Rayonier added from 4-6-0 #18, which had been scrapped earlier.(Ken Schmelzer collection)

Above, after a heavy rain in the mid-'50s, the 111 prepares to take over a load from a diesel transport truck at the Crane Creek loading *platform. (Stan Kistler photo, Paul Pauly collection)*

Above, the 111 at Railroad Camp in 1955 not long after its arrival from Weyerhaeuser at Longview, Washington. (Al Farrow collection)

Below, with cylinder cocks open, the 111 pulls out of Railroad Camp to begin her day's work. Note the wheelsets in the foreground. (Al Farrow collection)

Above, the 111 supplying steam to the car shop at Railroad Camp. (Al Farrow collection)

Below, No. 120 at Railroad Camp. The paint on the front of her smokebox will soon be re-applied.(H.G. Nelson photo, William D. Jones collection)

Above, performing double duty as engineer, Trainmaster Paul Pauly glides the 120 across the Axford Prairie crossing on the way to Log City. (Stan Kistler photo, Paul Pauly collection)

Below, steam up to the top, squirrel tails at the pops, and rods flapping, Buster Corrigan speeds the 120

through Axford Prairie with a load of goods headed for Log City. (Stan Kistler photo, Buster Corrigan collection)

Above, the No. 14, bell ringing and whistle blowing, emerges from early morning fog as she approaches the main 101 crossing at Axford Prairie. Buster Corrigan is at the throttle in this March 1961 photo. (D.R. Anderson photo,

Buster Corrigan collection)

Below, Engineer Buster Corrigan brings old No. 14 southbound from Crane Creek to Railroad Camp with 50 loads of freshly cut timber.

He is just about to cross the west fork of the Stevens River near Humptulips. (Buster Corrigan collection)

Above, the old trestle is being torn down in the background as No. 14 hauls loads of ballast in cars leased from the Northern Pacific. (Al Farrow collection)

Below, No. 14 performs some switching chores at Camp 14. Note the new barrel spark arrester on her stack and the added air pump she was given after her move from

Sekiu to Railroad Camp. This lokey is a sister to No. 120 and the Sierra. (Al Farrow collection)

Above, Mallet No. 14 hauls a long
load through Axford Prairie, on her
way to the log dump at New
London. (H.G. Nelson photo,
William D. Jones collection)

Below, the No. 99, a Baldwin 2-8-0,
at an unknown location. (H.G.
Nelson photo, Rayonier collection)

Below, on an unusually sunny day in May 1960 the Sierra, with squirrel tails at her pops, comes pounding up the grade at Promised Land, with a long load of empties headed for Crane Creek. Saved from the scrappers' torch, this famous lokey is on display at Crane Creek today. (Al Farrow collection)

Above, waiting on a siding for clearance to return to Railroad Camp, Engineer Clark Pennick checks the Sierra's running gear while Fireman John Wickman

minds the office. (Stan Kistler photo, Paul Pauly collection)

Below, the famed Sierra, replete with perennial steam leaks, brings

a load through Axford Prairie. The main line rail sits on good, ballasted roadbed. (H.G. Nelson photo, William D. Jones collection)

Above, in June of 1959 the 38, Walschaerts flapping, paddles across the No. 5 grade crossing just before the line was relocated for safety reasons (Al Farrow collection)

Below, the Sierra, sanding her flues, crosses the old Prairie River bridge in 1959. This trestle was later torn down and a new steel deck bridge was erected next to it. (Al Farrow collection)

Above, a wet No. 38 trudges across the newly rebuilt Humptulips bridge. In the background under the bridge are some of the wood pilings left from the old bridge. (Stan Kistler photo, Paul Pauly collection)

Below, the Sierra on her last run for Rayonier, bringing her load down across the new Humptulips bridge to Railroad Camp. At Axford Praire she will turn the train over to the No. 90, which will in turn hand the load over to a

new diesel, for the final leg of the journey to New London. (Al Farrow collection)

Top, a variation of the skeleton cars, these log carriers have a much wider center sill and wide decking over the trucks. They were acquired from the Port Angeles & Western Railroad. The builder is unknown. Note that car No. 932 utilizes "cheese blocks"—pieces of iron forged into a triangle which was threaded with chain to secure the logs. The car behind it is equipped with tall vertical arms called "stakes," a newer development. (Ken Schmelzer collection)

Center, the unusual swivel-bunk cars built by Rayonier using Pacific Car & Foundry parts were used for hauling long logs, either piling or "boomsticks." They were usually used in pairs as the "swivel" was just on one end of the car.

This load of timber is about to be dumped at the New London log dump. The left rail of the disconnect's track is elevated slightly to help the logs roll off. Note that this particular high truck has an iron strap broken just above the coupler. The steam-powered unloader on the left track was constructed at Railroad Camp. (H.G. Nelson photo, Rayonier collection)

Below, to dump the logs, chains securing the logs to the skeletons were released, and a hook was attached underneath the load of logs. A cable was then attached to the hook, and the crane arm, powered by steam, raised up into the air until the cable was stretched tight. That forced the logs to be thrust towards the edge of the car until they toppled over into the water. (H.G. Nelson photo, Rayonier collection)

Above, trainmaster Paul Pauly gets clearance for the Sierra to head up to the woods. Operations became more efficient after the switch from telephones to two-way radios, since the radios allowed continuous communication, rather than waiting for an engineer to get to a telephone station out in the woods and call back to the office at Railroad Camp. (Stan Kistler photo, Paul Pauly collection)

Below, the track gang lays new, heavier rail on the main line at Humptulips to accommodate diesel locomotives. Bob Hattan is at the helm of the crane. (Al Farrow collection)

In July of 1972, diesels No. 76 and 90, on the head end of a string of 70 loads, hit some rain-softened turf and derailed. The 90 didn't go all the way over, but during the course of the clean-up operations the following day, the vibrations of the equipment got her moving and she, too, almost went clear over on her side. Again, there was no serious injury either to crews or equipment (All photos: Buster Corrigan collection)

A pile driver is in the process of constructing a low trestle to reach a new logging site not too far north of Hoquiam. Women (posing in front of the Ten-spot) *were a rare sight out in the woods. (H.G. Nelson photo, Rayonier collection)*

Above, just in from a day's work, the 120 and No. 90 sit in a light rain at Railroad Camp. (Bill Jones photo, Rayonier collection)

Below, Mikado No. 90, now on display in Garibaldi, Oregon, edges past the 120 as she pulls out of Railroad Camp after a rain. (H.G. Nelson photo, William D. Jones collection)

Above, lokeys 90, 45 (in shed), and the Two-spot at Railroad Camp early in 1958. Note the hand car at the far right (Al Farrow collection)

Below, a row of husky Mallets guard the engine shed at Railroad Camp in May of 1959. (Al Farrow collection)

Open House
Signals the End

On March 31, 1962 an open house was held at Railroad Camp to commemorate the official end of the steam era. Steam lokeys continued to be used as back-up power, however, until the last lokey was run in 1967. (Al Farrow collection)

Above, Shay No. 3, carrying a steam donkey, on display at Promised Land Park on Highway 101 north of Humptulips. (H.G. Nelson photo, William D. Jones collection)

*The No. 45, a 2-6-2
Baldwin, was one of the earlier
lokeys to work the woods. It now
sits on display in downtown
Hoquiam. (H.G. Nelson photo,
William D. Jones collection)*

111

AMP G.
MP 3.

55

112

Chapter Four
In the Woods

The logging spurs saw no first-class high iron. Lokeys were small and light, and the track was makeshift at best. Rails were laid on rough-hewn ties, on a roughed-out railbed, for the lokeys to navigate as best they could. The very earliest track was even laid down over modified skid roads. Until the 1920s and early '30s, when heavier lokeys required more substantial track and good, solid roadbed, the life cycle of a logging spur was fairly simple: rough ties were slapped down onto the muddy ground, small lokeys—Climaxes, Heislers and light Shays—hauled their daily loads of six or seven disconnects until the spur area played out, then the track was either pulled out and taken to a new location or just left behind to rust.

Logging the spurs was an operation that required not only specialized equipment, but a unique crew as well. These men lived a rugged life, and their only home while logging was a cold, damp bunkhouse mounted atop a skeleton car. Living arrangements were necessarily spartan. The bunkhouse provided a place to sleep and a roof overhead, and that was about it. A well-run camp provided plenty of warm food and good fellow crew members. There were some bad operations out there, too, but they had constant trouble keeping crews. Men worked for them long enough to find out what they were like, then left for better camps—although none of the camps was paradise. There seemed to be only two types of days for a logger: overcast or rainy. In the fall and winter months it drizzled or rained almost daily and no one was spared the perils of muck, slimy moss and fingers too cold and stiff to obey the brain's commands. Gripping cold and long hours, plus the dangers of falling trees, loose footing, various mechanical accidents and even bears invading camp spelled the logger's life—a life which you somehow had to love in order to tolerate at all. But the loggers learned the dangers and coped with them.

The train crew had their share of difficulties as well. Trying to get trains safely up and down the spurs, transferring to the main lines, and handling wet appliances was no easy task. In the early days there was no such thing as automatic air brakes. The brakeman, or "brakie," had to run alongside a slow-moving train—through an obstacle course of mud, wet sticks, and slick leaves—and tie down the brakes on the disconnects. Steel wheels on wet steel rails didn't stop readily, and it wasn't uncommon for a brakie to loose his footing and slide a mile or so down the track with a slow runaway. He either regained his footing somehow and tied down the trucks, or the train picked up momentum and trouble was on its way. Back when lokeys were light and loads were short, a runaway could still be managed. Trains didn't run very fast—maybe five to eight miles per hour—and if trouble arose, the engineer had time to shut her down, lay on the steam jammer until the brakie caught up and tied down a disconnect, and the whole show slid to a halt. If the train derailed or dumped a log, it was going too slow to do any real damage—the only loss was usually in time and labor. As Hattan says, though, "It was certainly touchy stuff. You can imagine the brakeman had to be pretty fast because of the worn brake blocks and hickeys, and if he missed it, well, that was that. Away she'd go! Even though the lokey had the jammer, you had to bleed her all the time or she'd start priming and that was the end of your brakes right now." Later, as the lokeys got bigger and loads grew longer and heavier, stopping a train became more complicated. Man was no match for the laws of physics—a heavy runaway was more costly and infinitely more dangerous to life and limb.

Engineer Buster Corrigan knew the spurs as well as anyone: "I began running those lokeys in 1927 at

(H.G. Nelson photo, Rayonier collection)

the age of 18 for the Saginaw Timber Company, and then in 1934 I came over to the Polson operations. Hell, I'd have stayed at Saginaw, but I knew the old man real well, and well, we'd get into arguments so many times and I'd get mad and quit, and then he'd hire me back and I'd go, of course. But as time went on, and Polson was building, I knew lots of crews up there, so I just up and went. Now, since I was a 'hill man' and knew how to handle those lokeys on them grades, the Polson people had me running everything they had. Mac Polson, Alex's nephew, fired with me many times and was a good tallowpot, too. I ran the Two-spot on the Saginaw, which was a sister to Polson's No. 101, which I ran here since I knew her type so well. She lasted a long time and was a good lokey right up until she was scrapped. Later, when they started buying up all the Mallets, I ran all of 'em. One time I was running the 99 down with a load of disconnects and Clayton Reese, my brakeman, had started out to tie the trucks down and these things had square holes where you put your hickey in and started twisting the brakes on. Well, the hole had been worn and when Clayton started to bind up the shoes, his hickey flipped out and onto the ground. Well, that was the end of that! We came down the hill doing about 25 or 30 with a load, and came upon a section crew, and went flying through there like hell bent for election. They took off for the woods in every direction and of course later filed a complaint to the 'super' about us coming through so fast. I simply told him what had happened and that there was nothing we could do about it with what we had to work with. Later 'Peggy' Rogers, one of our engineers, and Bennet Ellingston, our superintendent, along with Mac Polson, started buying up all the skeleton log cars they could find. These cars had air on them and solved all the runaway problems."

Apart from the loggers, train crews were a breed of their own. You had to be in love with trains—their mystery, their fascination, the smell of smoke, oil and steam. Logging was secondary to the railroad boys. You also had to love this type of railroading, far different from the mainline operations of the big road names. The advantages were mostly intangible—the freedom of working your own train without the mounds of rules and regulations that seemed to engulf the freight and passenger outfits, and the pride of being part of a special team. Logging operations offered a new and different challenge that couldn't be matched on the main lines. Here in the woods everyone from the camp cook to the whistle punk took per-

sonal pride in his work and his equipment. There is a special camaraderie among the crews—the respect they have for each other is remarkable and friendships developed on the job frequently last for years. They wouldn't be human, though, if disagree-

ments didn't occur form time to time. Arguments in the bunkhouse—after a long, hard day of back-breaking labor—sometimes led to swinging fists, but altercations were soon forgotten and it was back to business as usual. Although logging, railroading and individual crew members have changed, human nature has not. The crews are as fascinating as the job they perform, and the unique breed of Rayonier crews remains much the same today.□

Above, chaining up a log on a pair of disconnects out in the woods. In the background is a steam donkey equipped with a rain shelter. Note the lack of ballasted roadbed under the rails. (H.G. Nelson photo, Rayonier collection)

Below, "taking five" at Camp 4. (H.G. Nelson photo, Rayonier collection)

Above, a look at Camp 4, with
bunkhouses lined up along a spur
in the background, and two swing
donkeys at work, in the early
1900s. (H.G. Nelson photo,

Rayonier collection)
Below, decades would pass before
automatic washing machines
would find their way into camp.
These hands had to build up a fire

to heat water fetched from the river
before tossing in their duds. For all
their work, the clothes didn't stay
clean for long. (H.G. Nelson photo,
Rayonier collection)

Above, in front of the bunkhouse sits a pair of skeleton cars with steel I-beam bunks and chocks. Replacing primitive disconnects, these cars were equipped with air brakes (note rigging underneath) and ushered in a safer era of logging by rail. (Ken Schmelzer collection)

Right, at an unknown location, the duty cook poses with his family for this early '20s photo. These bunks—the original "mobile homes"—were set up on flat cars rather than on disconnects, as was the usual practice. Tacked to the door frame is the cook's time card. (H.G. Nelson photo, Rayonier collection)

Above, the No. 120 heads a train of logs through typical dense Olympic Peninsula timberland.

Below, the hefty three-truck Shay No. 91 pulls a load of logs down from a spur in November 1941. (H.G. Nelson photo, William D. Jones collection)

At an unidentified location in the woods, a hastily-built pole bridge spans a picturesque creek on the way to the log dump. Certainly not approved by the yet-to-be-established Association of American Railroads, these bridges nevertheless withstood years of heavy loads. (H.G. Nelson photo, Rayonier collection)

Chapter Five
The Men and the Machines

In the early days the geared lokeys did the chores in the woods and the light 2-6-2s, Ten Wheelers and 2-8-0s worked the main line to New London. Wood was the fuel of choice—after all, there was plenty of it around—while Bunker C oil was relatively new, except to the main line boys. During the war years of 1916-1918, however, the need for Washington's strong, lightweight spruce to support the building of aircraft was urgent, and other woods were badly needed for building. This necessitated the purchase of more cars, engines and support equipment. It was during these years that Bunker C oil was allocated and engines No. 70, 90, 99 and 101—all oil burners—joined the team, and the smaller lokeys were converted to oil burners. This not only relieved the crews assigned to cut and load the cords of wood each day, but also alleviated a fire hazard, as the heavy oil didn't throw out sparks like wood did.

During the '20s and '30s, with the War off and the Depression on, production backed off in the woods, along with other segments of the economy. Rayonier, however, still continued its ongoing research of pulp products and chemicals, and it concentrated heavily in these areas. With the advent of new materials and processes, the company managed to get through the grim years until the need for wood picked up once again. The Polson Brothers Logging Company, in the meantime, was still logging spruce and Douglas fir for the military, and shingles for housing, which kept them going until Rayonier bought the company out. After the merger, Nos. 110, 111, 14, 38 and 120 were put on the roster to handle the increased tonnage.

Disconnects were still in use, but only behind smaller lokeys. The larger Mallets handled the regular log cars, mostly surplus bought from other operations that had gone by the wayside or had reduced production. "Before Rayonier came in," Mac Polson said, "we used Shays, Climaxes, and small rod lokeys, and our mainline stuff was small Mikes and Prairies. We had all sorts of rolling stock on the line—disconnects, truss rod flats, homemade gons for work trains, and hundreds of skeleton log bunks that old Bennet Ellingston and I scoured the country for. We bought everything we could find, and had a menagerie of odd-sized cars all over the property. Some of them had 3-ft.-wide beams, some with 30-in. beams and all manner of drawbars on them, but with small loads and hoggers [who were] used to them, [it] wasn't much of a problem. But when the 3100 tied onto these with a long train, she'd pull them apart. The train crew would have to block all the loads with the broad beams at the head end, with the narrower cars at the rear, and then really jockey that Mallet to get her going and not pull the train apart. Hell, she'd pull the whole camp out if you had a chain big enough to hold around it!" Eventually they began phasing out the old disconnects, though, and replacing them with newer cars equipped with air brakes, ushering in a new, safer era of logging.

The Rayonier operation was now a modern-day show, with safety and efficiency rivaling the mainline operations. The crews kept the equipment in top condition and the lokeys were constantly maintained, kept clean and shiny. Hostler Bob Hattan said he could have kept a full-time cotton mill in operation just providing the rags! "I learned how to run those old slobber-stacked saturated steam lokeys from my dad on the Donovan Corkery operation. Even when I came to Rayonier, the boys used to tell me about those old slobber stacks, the early one like we had at Donovan. They would blow sludge, soot, and wet, greasy steam all over the place and boy, was that stuff hard to clean off! Even after I came to work at Rayonier, we had a few of those old birds there, and I had to clean those jackets down on the weekend for the next week's work, and it was just a hell of a job to clean that gunk off the oiler. If an engineer was good, and knew that he had one, he'd usually back the engine down slowly and let all the gunk out of the stack fall onto the track ahead of him before the morning run. Sometimes, though, they'd forget or be in a hurry, and blow that gunk all over the boiler, and the hostler had to wipe the whole engine down the next day or that night for the next run. Rayonier took great pride in their lokeys and insisted on good-looking, clean engines. Before I got the crane duty, I hired out as a fireman and hostler and had the duty of cleaning and setting up the lokeys for the weekly runs and they still had that 3100 on the property and she was without a doubt the dirtiest grime bucket I ever had anything to do with!"

But as the years wore on, so did the lokeys. Demands of the World War II took their toll, and despite top-notch maintenance crews, the aging lokeys began breaking down and repairs became more frequent. The able men who built, repaired and maintained the lokeys aged, too. As they retired, finding knowledgeable replacements became increasingly difficult, and by this time spare parts were almost impossible to locate. Fortunately for Rayonier, however, there were still a few of the old-timers on the property who could maintain the equipment. They continued to do so on into the '60s, maintaining, rebuilding, and even forging and casting their own parts when necessary to keep the old lokeys running. As the '60s arrived, many of the earlier lokeys had long since worn out and been scrapped, and even the hardy main line Mallets were beginning to see the end coming. The old steam donkeys had all been replaced with newer diesel equipment, bulldozers had taken over up on the spurs, and modern, diesel-powered loaders were now unloading logs from diesel trucks to the last remaining main line at Crane Creek.

Making do with what was there applied to men as well as machines. Each man learned from other crew members how to perform as many different functions as necessary so the show could go on even if someone got sick or injured. Paul Pauly adds, "I'd done a little bit of everything, I guess, in the years that I worked for the early log outfits, but got most of my experience on the old Donovan Corkery road where I learned to fire and brake and even finally run the lokeys, and worked there until I came to Rayonier. However, in 1940 I ruptured a disc up in the woods picking up a log load, and could no longer work the train. That's how I got involved dispatching and later, in about 1944, became trainmaster of the line. One time just before I came to Rayonier, while still at Donovan, the Simpson Company had a big fire and one of the brakemen got his thumb cut off during the battle, and they called me over to work

the fire titan. Like most of the crews, all of us ran the lokeys or fired them at one time or another, whether you were a brakeman, craneman, or what, so you always had someone around to do the job when needed. We didn't have unions in the early days and you had to be a jack of all trades. I ran the 45 a lot and the 90 sometimes, but mostly in the yards at Railroad Camp. Hell, I worked with all of the old crews: Peggy Rogers, Leo McCabe, Clark Pennick, Bennet Ellingston, who was my boss, and even Mickey the Rat." Bob Hattan had a similar background: "My Dad, 'Rip' Hattan, worked for Donovan and got me on there with him as a brakeman and then I learned to fire and run and that's how I later came to Rayonier. I was to take a job as hogger, but wound up on the crane because of my background with diesel and electric equipment while in the Navy. I did a stint with my dad at Donovan until about 1934, and things began to drop off at Donovan, so I went to Rayonier then and hired on as a hostler. I did just about everything, though, but run trains. I was a mechanic, hostler, ground man and all that stuff before I finally became the duty crane operator. My dad gave me a book to read, *The Engineman's Manual*, but you still had to go out on the road and learn by practical experience."

Mac Polson began as a construction boss setting up the Prairie Creek branch and was head scaler at Railroad Camp and later at Camp 14. Over the years he fired the 101, 18, 70, the Shays 91, 191, and 55, the 3 and Ten-spots, and even Ol' Betsy. "Ol' 'Fat' Gable taught me how to fire, and he was a hell of a good fireman and spent many years on the 101 in the woods. Fat said to me one day when I was just getting my boots dirty, 'Mac,' he said, 'No two lokeys are the same, and no two hoggers are, either. Some of those hoggers you had to be a week ahead of, and others you could be a week behind, and still catch up to them if you had to. If you aren't careful that hogger will pull the fire out from under you and walk away until you got her back in again.' Fat worked with a hogger named Nestor in the old days on the 101 and Peggy Rogers ran the No. 70 from the time she came on the property till he retired. Peggy was one of those hoggers you had to be a week ahead of, too. Hell, he was clever with his hands. He'd work all the valves and levers on his side of the cab all the time, and you had to stay with him on your side or you were in a pile of trouble. He'd slip that old lokey up to a string of logs, pull the Johnson bar over just as the coupler would hit the string and have that lokey locked up and pulling the slack without even stopping the engine. I never saw a man run an engine so smooth. He was smooth as hell,' Fat would say, and you really had to stay with him or get kicked off his lokey. Old Crawgstead was Peggy's fireman, and stayed with him for years, and of course, was one of the best, too. You had to be to work with Peggy."

By now, almost all the old-timers are gone—some retired, and some gone to that great logging show in the sky—and the old shops like Baldwin and Lima are found only in history books. But the new bunch today has the same problems of making do with what they have in order to keep the trains rolling. Lew Rowe, who now is the man in charge of maintenance, still has the chores of rebuilding, repairing and keeping the old log cars in shape as did his predecessor, Ralph Endressen. Today, though, instead of crown sheets, boiler tubes, flues, and drivers, it's diesel engine parts, traction motors to be repaired, and steel I-beams to be replaced on the log cars. The new breed at Rayonier is just as capable with their modern equipment and the technology of today as the old-timers were with theirs. But they all say steam was an era of challenge, price and conquest.

I would like to have been there, but man, it was hard work! □

After a day's run Bobby Rogers, left, and his father, Peggy Rogers, pose on the pilot of the No. 90. Father-son teams were not unusual in the logging and rail camps. (Stan Kistler photo, Paul Pauly collection)

125

Left, part of the Railroad Camp crew, including a boy, a dog, and the kitchen staff, pose in front of wood-burning Shay No. 33, still outfitted with a shotgun stack, for a group portrait. The wool coats were quite heavy—even heavier when wet—mildewed easily, and took forever to dry, especially in the rain forest. What a blessing lightweight, waterproof and rip-proof synthetics would have been. All the people in this photo are very likely gone by now—except, perhaps, for the very young man with the toy horse in his lap. (H.G. Nelson photo, Rayonier collection)

Inset, Shay No. 33, outfitted with a new oil bunker, sets up a train on the main line. (H.G. Nelson photo, Rayonier collection)

LIMA LOCOMOTIVE WORKS, INCORPORATED
LIMA, OHIO

Class: Pacific Coast Shay Geared

Road No. 11

GAUGE OF TRACK	DRIVING WHEEL DIAMETER	FUEL KIND	CYLINDERS			BOILER		FIREBOX	
			NO.	DIAMETER	STROKE	DIAMETER	PRESSURE	LENGTH	WIDTH
4'-8½"	36"	OIL	3	13"	15"	50⅛"	200 LBS.	89¼"	44¾"

WHEEL BASE			MAXIMUM TRACTIVE POWER	FACTOR OF ADHESION	TUBES AND FLUES		
TRUCK	ENGINE	ENGINE AND TENDER			NUMBER	DIAMETER	LENGTH
4'-4"	30'-8"	41'-2"	38200	4.74	97 / 15	2" / 5¾"	11'-0"

AVERAGE WEIGHT IN WORKING ORDER, POUNDS		GRATE AREA SQ. FT.	HEATING SURFACES, SQUARE FEET			
ON DRIVERS	TOTAL ENGINE		TUBES AND FLUES	FIREBOX	TOTAL	SUPER-HEATER
181000	181000	27.75	783	122	905	189

Capacity, Water 3000 Gallons

Fuel 1200 Gals.

Baldwin 2-8-0 No. 99 chugs down a grade from Camp 7. She was later converted to burn Bunker C oil, and was scrapped in 1948. (H.G. Nelson photo, Rayonier collection)

During World War II the crews in the woods also kept watch for enemy planes. Here trainmaster Paul Pauly, seated, and Bob Ellis *pose for an Air Force photographer. In the background is the track board used to locate trains during their runs. (Official* *United States Air Force photo, Paul Pauly collection)*

*Above, the No. 45, a Baldwin
2-6-2, dumps a load at New
London. This lokey was built in
1906 and is on display in
Hoquiam, Washington. (H.G.
Nelson photo, Rayonier collection)*

Above, as the crews arrive at Railroad Camp from a day's work up in the woods, the next order of business is dinner. The hands at camp usually ate before or after the railroad boys. In this 1953 photo, it looks as though Bennet Ellingston, in doorway, Paul Pauly, on step, and the camp dog have already had a good meal. (Stan Kistler photo, Paul Pauly collection)

Left, pop valve detail on the No. 120. (Buster Corrigan collection)

Right, pop valve detail on the No. 38. (Buster Corrigan collection)

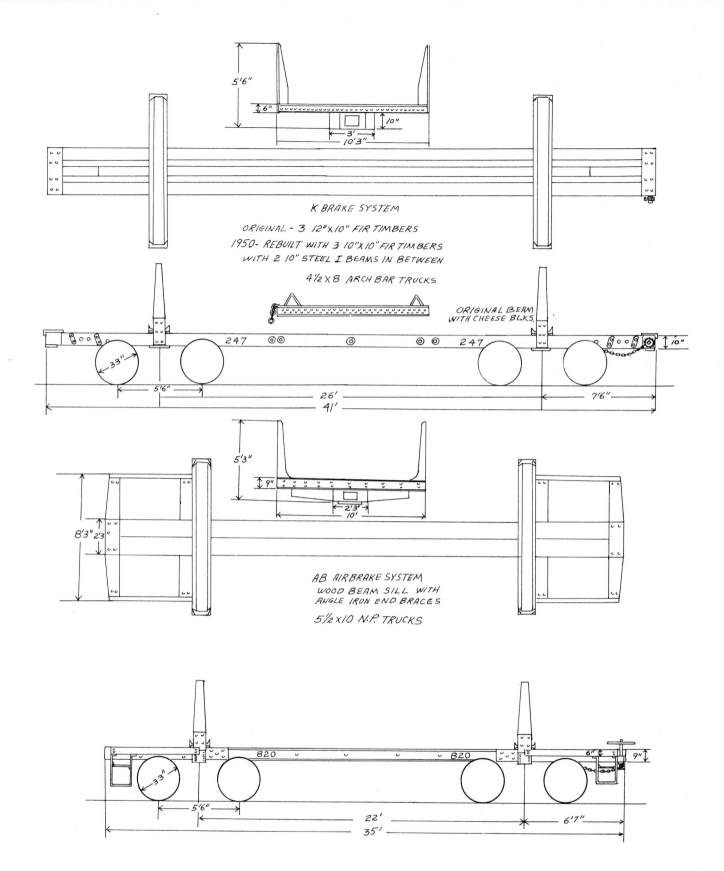

K BRAKE SYSTEM

ORIGINAL - 3 12"x10" FIR TIMBERS

1950- REBUILT WITH 3 10"x10" FIR TIMBERS
WITH 2 10" STEEL I BEAMS IN BETWEEN

4½ X 8 ARCH BAR TRUCKS

ORIGINAL BEAM
WITH CHEESE BLKS.

AB AIRBRAKE SYSTEM
WOOD BEAM SILL WITH
ANGLE IRON END BRACES

5½ X 10 N.P. TRUCKS

Rayonier Logging Cars

Drawn J. Spencer 1979
From original Rayonier plans

132

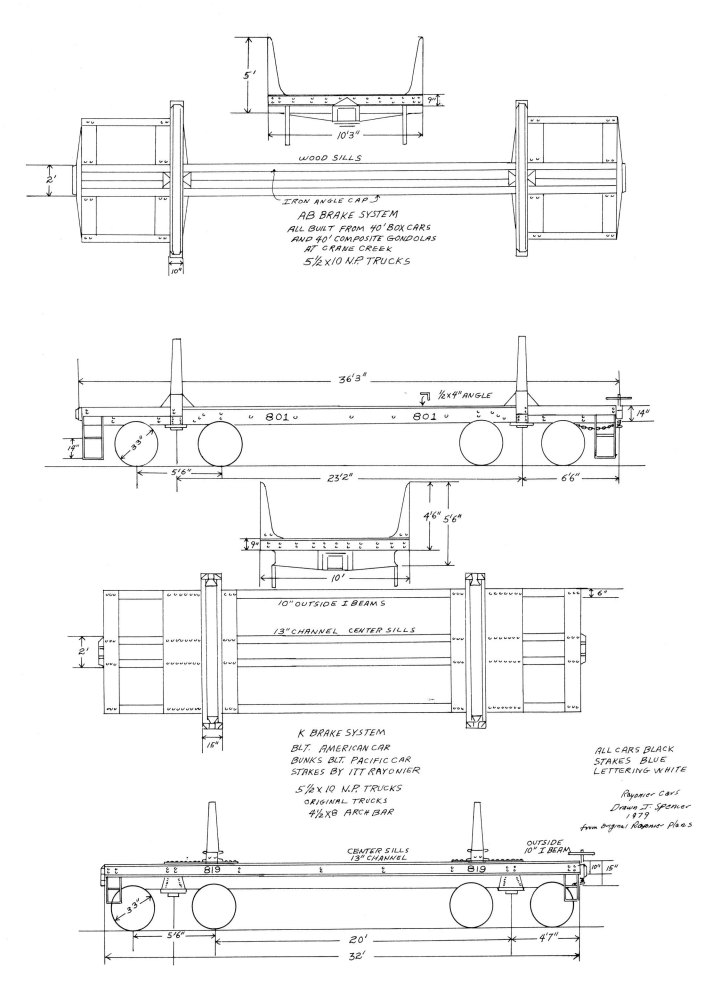

WOOD SILLS

IRON ANGLE CAP

AB BRAKE SYSTEM
ALL BUILT FROM 40' BOX CARS
AND 40' COMPOSITE GONDOLAS
AT CRANE CREEK
5½ X 10 N.P. TRUCKS

36'3"

½ X 4" ANGLE

801   801

33"

5'6"   23'2"   6'6"

14"

10" OUTSIDE I BEAMS

13" CHANNEL CENTER SILLS

4'6" 5'6"

6"

15"

K BRAKE SYSTEM
BLT. AMERICAN CAR
BUNKS BLT. PACIFIC CAR
STAKES BY ITT RAYONIER

5½ X 10 N.P. TRUCKS
ORIGINAL TRUCKS
4½ X 8 ARCH BAR

ALL CARS BLACK
STAKES BLUE
LETTERING WHITE

Rayonier Cars
Drawn J. Spencer
1979
from original Rayonier plans

CENTER SILLS
13" CHANNEL

OUTSIDE
10" I BEAM

819   819

10" 15"

33"

5'6"   20'   4'7"

32'

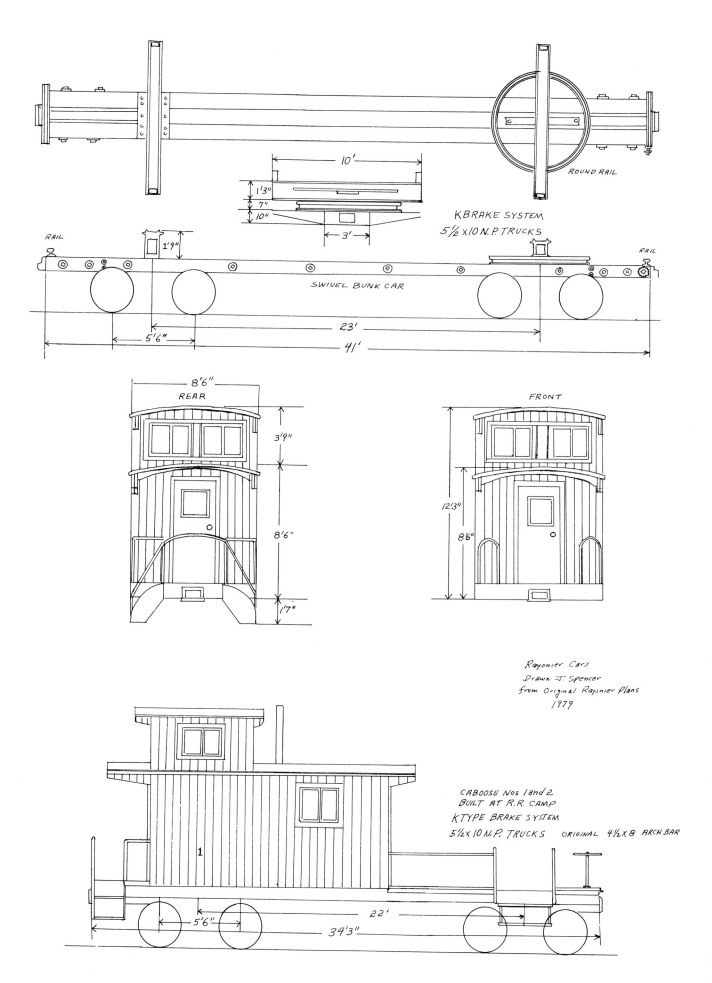

ROUND RAIL

KBRAKE SYSTEM
5½ X 10 N.P. TRUCKS

10'

1'3"
7"
10"

3'

RAIL

1'9"

SWIVEL BUNK CAR

RAIL

5'6"

23'

41'

8'6"
REAR

3'9"

8'6"

1'7"

FRONT

12'3"

8'6"

Rayonier Cars
Drawn J. Spencer
from Original Rayonier Plans
1979

CABOOSE Nos 1 and 2
BUILT AT R.R. CAMP
K TYPE BRAKE SYSTEM
5½ X 10 N.P. TRUCKS   ORIGINAL 4½ X 8 ARCH BAR

1

5'6"

22'

34'3"

RAYONIER № 8

Hostler Bob Hattan readies the
110 for the day's work.
(Paul Pauly collection)

(Roy Peacher photo)

At left, only a trained eye would see that this is not the real Rayonier No. 70, but a faithful live-steam reproduction (1½ inch to the foot) expertly built by David Skagen of Shelton, Washington. (Pete Replinger photo, David Skagen collection)

Above, Skagen, who actually fired the full-sized No. 70, says his model will work just as hard as the big one and even sounds the same. (David Skagen collection)

Some of the men who made things go. Bennet Ellingston, superintendent of Railroad Camp (Max Wexler drawings)

Bobby Rogers, engineer and son of Peggy Rogers

Adrian Juius, master mechanic and *Al McCleod, boilermaker.*

Left, after serving Bloedel-Donovan and Rayonier for several years, the Eight-spot was sold to Puget Sound Railway Historical Association members Byron Cole and Pete Replinger and is now stored near Shelton, Washington awaiting overhaul. (Pete Replinger photo, David Skagen collection)
Above, engineer Buster Corrigan at the throttle. (Buster Corrigan collection)

STEAM LOCOMOTIVE ROSTER

NO.	WHEEL ARR.	TYPE	BUILDER	SERIAL NUMBER	DATE	DRIVERS (INCHES)	CYLINDERS (INCHES)
GRAYS HARBOR OPERATION							
2	2-8-2	Mikado	Baldwin	38967	1912	44	18x24
3	2-Truck	Shay	Lima	2305	1910	26½	8x8
10	4-6-0	Ten Wheeler	Baldwin				
18	4-6-0	Ten Wheeler	Baldwin	18734	1901		
33	2-Truck	Shay	Lima	1614	1905	32	11x12
38	2-6-6-2	Articulated	Baldwin	61781	1934	51	20x3x28
45	2-6-2	Prairie	Baldwin	23311	1906	44	15x24
51	2-8-0	Consolidation	Baldwin	10447	1889		
55	2-Truck	Shay	Lima	1959	1907	32	12x12
70	2-8-2	Mikado	Baldwin	55355	1922	44	18x24
90	2-8-2	Mikado	Baldwin	59071	1926	48	20x28
91	3-Truck	Shay	Lima	3322	1928	36	13x15
99	2-8-0	Consolidation	Baldwin	25416	1905	50	20x24
101	2-8-2	Mikado	Baldwin	38966	1912	44	18x24
110	2-6-6-2T	Articulated	Baldwin	60561	1928	44	17x26x2
111	2-6-6-2T	Articulated	Baldwin	62064	1937	44	18x28x2
120	2-6-6-2	Articulated	Baldwin	61904	1936	51	20x31x2
191	3-Truck	Shay	Lima	3343	1929	36	13x15
3100	2-6-6-2	Articulated	Baldwin	34389	1910	55	20x31x3

WEIGHT	TRACTIVE EFFORT	PRESSURE (P.S.I.)	REMARKS
141,150	27,000	180	Ex-Saginaw Lumber No. 2. Sold to Grand Traverse; then Cadillac Lake City RR; then Kettle Moraine. Now (1998) Mid-Continent Railway Musem.
48,000	10,700	160	Ex-Kootenay Logging No. 2; ex-Polson No. 3. To display at Promised Land Park, then Polson Museum. Now Mt. Rainier Scenic Railroad.
no details			Ex-UP. Scrapped at Railroad Camp in 1955.
110,000	no details		Bought from Baldwin-Weisbaum in 1918. Originally built for Arizona New Mexico Railroad.
90,000			Scrapped at Railroad Camp in 1947.
293,000	59,600	225	Ex-Weyerhaeuser No. 4; ex-Sierra No. 38. Now on display at Crane Creek.
88,600	16,700	180	Ex-Polson No. 45. To display at Historic Park, Hoquiam. Now Mt. Rainier Scenic Railroad.
180,000	no details		Ex-NP No. 51. Received in trade for Ol' Betsy in 1933.
110,000			Scrapped at Railroad Camp in 1948 after wrecked in runaway.
141,150	27,000	180	Ex-Polson No. 70. To Puget Sound Railroad Historical Society, Snoqualmie Falls. Now Mt. Rainier Scenic Railroad.
185,100	35,700	180	Ex-Polson No. 90. Now on display at Oregon Memorial Steam Train Association in Garibaldi, Oregon.
181,000	38,200	200	Ex-Polson 91. Sold to Georgia Pacific, Oroville, California in 1958; then to Feather River Railway for parts.
137,000	29,200	180	Ex-Polson No. 99. Scrapped at Railroad Camp in 1959.
141,150	27,100	180	Ex-Polson No. 101. Scrapped at Railroad Camp in 1959.
222,000	37,500	200	Ex-Weyerhaeuser first No. 110. Sold to National Railroad Historical Society, Promontory, Utah Chapter in 1968, then Wasatch Museum, now Nevada State RR Museum.
247,000	42,500	200	Ex-Weyerhaeuser second No. 110. Sold to California Western Railroad at Fort Bragg, California, #46. Saddle tanks removed. Now at San Diego Railroad Museum.
293,000	59,600	220	Ex-Weyerhaeuser No. 120; ex-Chehalis Western No. 120. Sister to No. 38. Scrapped at Railroad Camp in 1968.
188,500	38,200	200	Ex-Polson No. 191. Sold to Georgia Pacific, Oroville, California in 1958. Believed now scrapped.
305,150	58,000	210	Ex-NP No. 3100; ex-Polson No. 3100. Scrapped at Railroad Camp in 1959.

(Al Farrow photos)

NO.	WHEEL ARR.	TYPE	BUILDER	SERIAL NUMBER	DATE	DRIVERS (INCHES)	CYLINDER (INCHES)
CLALLAM BRANCH							
1	3-Truck	Climax	Climax	1648	1924	36	15¼x16
2(1)	3-Truck	Shay	Lima	2908	1917	33	12x15
2(2)	3-Truck	Willamette	Willamette	34	1929	36	12½x15
3(1)	3-Truck	Shay	Lima	2786	1914	36	13½x15
3(2)	3-Truck	Willamette	Willamette	20	1926	36	12x15
4	3-Truck	Willamette	Willamette	16	1924	36	12x15
5	3-Truck	Shay	Lima	2855	1916	36	12x15
6	2-Truck	Heisler	Heisler	1288	1913	36	12x15
7	3-Truck	Shay	Lima	3012	1919	36	12x15
8	2-6-6-2T	Articulated	Baldwin	58064	1924	44	17x26x2
9	2-6-6-2T	Articulated	Baldwin	58065	1924	44	17x26x2
10(1)	3-Truck	Climax	Climax	1641	1923	36	15¼x16
10(2)	3-Truck	Shay	Lima	3348	1930	36	13x15
14	2-6-6-2	Articulated	Baldwin	60256	1927	51	20x31x2
15	3-Truck	Shay	Lima	3318	1928	36	13x15

WEIGHT	TRACTIVE EFFORT	PRESSURE (P.S.I.)	REMARKS
160,000	35,200	200	Ex-Bloedel Donovan No. 1. Scrapped by Owens Co., Port Angeles, in 1952.
157,000	33,100	200	Ex-Goodyear Lumber No. 2; ex-Bloedel Donovan No. 2. Scrapped by Owens in 1949.
182,000	34,687	200	Ex-J. Niels Lumber. Sold to Jim Gertz, Port Angeles. On display.
195,000	35,100	200	Ex-Goodyear Lumber No. 1; ex-Bloedel Donovan. Scrapped by Owens in 1950.
174,000	31,968	200	Ex-Ewauna Box Co. No. 103; ex-Weyco; Scrapped by Block & Co. in 1956.
174,000	31,968	200	Ex-Long-Bell Lumber Co. No. 701. Donated to the city of Port Angeles. On display.
140,000	30,350	200	Ex-Bloedel Donovan No. 5. Sold to Block & Co. Scrapped in 1955
188,000	18,800	180	Ex-Bloedel Donovan No. 6. Scrapped in 1944
140,000	30,350	200	Ex-Siems-Carey; ex-H.S. Kierbaugh Corp. No. 7; ex-Bloedel Donovan. Scrapped by Block & Co. in 1956.
212,500	37,500	200	Ex-Bloedel Donovan; currently owned by Byron Cole and Pete Replinger and stored near Shelton, Washington.
212,500	37,500	200	Ex-Bloedel Donovan. Sister to No. 8 Sold to Block & Co. and scrapped in 1958.
160,000	35,200	200	Ex-Bloedel Donovan Scrapped in 1947. Boiler sent to Hoko Camp for use as a heating plant.
188,800	38,200	200	Ex-Ozette Timber No. 10. Donated to the city of Forks, Washington in 1959. On display.
275,000	56,600	215	Ex-Larson Logging Co. No. 14; ex-Bloedel Donovan No. 14. Later moved to Grays Harbor line. Scrapped in 1968.
186,000	38,200	200	Ex-Bloedel Donovan No. 15. Sold to Block & Co. and scrapped in 1955.

(Al Farrow photos)

Above, Bloedel Donovan Lumber Mills three-truck Climax #1 at Sappho in 1939, prior to Rayonier ownership. Note steam fire pump on speeder—probably operated by air. (Harold A. Hill photo, Thomas Lawson, Jr. collection)

Below, the last run of Willamette #2 crosses Johnson Creek trestle in June of 1962. (Ken Schmelzer photo, Peter J. Replinger collection)

Above, Willamette #4 has a fresh coat of paint prior to being loaded on trucks and hauled to Port Angeles to be put on display in 1960. (Peter J. Replinger collection)

Below, Bloedel Donovon two-truck Heisler prior to Rayonier ownership. She was scrapped shortly after Rayonier took over. (Harold A Hill photo, Thomas Lawson Jr. collection)

Above, the 8-spot at the Lake Creek gravel pit. (Peter J. Replinger photo) Below, this is one of the last times steam was operated on the Clallam division—the third diesel arrived not long after. (Peter J. Replinger photo)

Above, 2-6-6-2T #9 taken at the log "transfer" at Soleduc in July, 1955, not long before the arrival of the diesels. (Peter J. Replinger collection)

Below, three-truck Climax #10 at Sappho prior to Rayonier owner-ship. (Harold A. Hill photo, Thomas Lawson Jr. collection)

DIESEL LOCOMOTIVE ROSTER

NO.	TYPE	BUILDER	SERIAL NUMBER	DATE	REMARKS
GRAYS HARBOR OPERATION					
14	AS616	B-L-H	#75357	1952	Originally Kaiser Steel #1012B, then #1028. To Trona RR #54. Then to Johnson Terminal (Okla.) Then to SLRS #554 (New Jersey) Now in use as SMS Rail Service.
45	AS616	B-L-H	#75469	5-1952	Purchased by Rayonier 12/61. (Numbered after 2-6-2 #45.) Originally Southern Pacific #5273. Scrapped.
70	AS616	B-L-H	#75468	2-1952	Originally Southern Pacific #5272. Purchased by Rayonier 11/67. (Numbered after 2-8-2 #70.) Scrapped.
76	AS616	B-L-H	#75472	5-1952	Originally Southern Pacific #5276. Purchased by Rayonier 1968. Scrapped.
90	AS616	B-L-H	#75471	5-1952	Originally Southern Pacific #5275. Purchased by Rayonier 12/61. (Numbered after 2-8-2 #90.) Scrapped.

Roster compiled by Pete Replinger 10/18/98
with help from Ken Ardinger and Jim Gertz.
All photos by Pete Replinger except where noted.

Left, Rayonier held an employee contest to design a color scheme for the Bicentennial. The results, won by a car shop employee, are shown here in September of 1975.

Left, below, the old and new side by side in Railroad Camp.

Left, two views of the little used diesel #14 sitting outside the shop at Crane Creek, in October of 1977.

Left, diesel #70 at Crane Creek in October of 1977.

Left, diesel #45 hauls a train through the woods.

DIESEL LOCOMOTIVE ROSTER

NO.	TYPE	BUILDER	SERIAL NUMBER	DATE	REMARKS
CLALLAM OPERATION					
201	S-12	B-L-H	#76136	7-1956	Purchased new. To U.S. Steel 2nd #36 (Geneva Works) Orem, Utah.
202	S-12	B-L-H	#76137	7-1956	Purchased new. To U.S. Steel 2nd #37 (Geneva Works) Orem, Utah.
203	S-12	B-L-H	#75912	10-1953	Originally McCloud River RR #30. Purchased Rayonier in 1963. To U.S. Steel (Pittsburg, CA 6/74, #16, then #76, then back to #16. To Portola-Feather River & Western, then resold McCloud Railroad.

Left, ex-McCloud diesel #203 poses outside the shops at Sekiu in September 1971.

Above and right, both #202 and #201 had water tanks installed on the running boards as a water supply for "railwashers" used for lubrication on the many curves prevelant on the Clallam operation.

Left, BLH S-12 #202 crosses Brown's Creek trestle on its way to the log dump at Sekiu, August 1970.

Below left and right, end of show at Sekiu, Septmber 1973. Locomotives are loaded on a barge, then towed to Tacoma where they were stored until purchased by new owners. Of the three S-12's, only the ex-McCloud unit (#203) exists today.

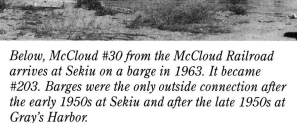

Below, McCloud #30 from the McCloud Railroad arrives at Sekiu on a barge in 1963. It became #203. Barges were the only outside connection after the early 1950s at Sekiu and after the late 1950s at Gray's Harbor.

Jim Gertz photo

Glossary

A-Frame: Timbers set up in the shape of the letter A with a block and cable at the top, used for lifting loads.

Air Brakes: Brakes on locomotives and rail cars which operate on compressed air and are controlled from the cab of the locomotive.

Arch Bar Trucks: A very early style of rail trucks made from shaped steel bars bolted together. This type preceded cast iron trucks.

Articulated Locomotive: A locomotive having two separate sets of drivers under one boiler. The rear set is in fixed alignment with the boiler while the front set can swivel from side to side, enabling the engine to negotiate tight curves.

Backhead: The rear of a locomotive boiler, on which various gauges, valves and accessories are mounted.

Ballast: Gravel or other hard material placed on the roadbed, which helps hold the ties in place and distributes the locomotive's weight more evenly. It also provides drainage.

Barstock: Lengths of iron or steel; the basic stock from which rail parts are forged.

Bind Up the Shoes: To set the brakes on a locomotive or rail car.

Bird: A locomotive.

Bogeys or Bogey Wheels: Another term for lead trucks and/or trailing trucks. Also *Bogies* or *Bogie Wheels*.

Boiler: The large cylindrical tank of a locomotive or donkey in which water is heated for conversion to steam.

Boiler Plate: The sheet steel from which the boiler of a locomotive or donkey is formed.

Bolster: The transverse beam of a truck or car frame which forms the bearing surface and joint between the two.

Bone Yard: The section of track set aside for derelict locomotives.

Boom: An A-frame carrying rigging used in loading.

Boomer: A worker who wandered from job to job.

Brakie: A brakeman. Also *Brakey*.

Bridles: Steel rods set between rails to keep them in gauge until they are spiked into place.

Brow Log: A heavy log set beside the track at the loading dock, to prevent logs from rolling against the cars or falling off onto the track.

Bucker: A woodsman who cuts logs into shorter lengths.

Bullcook: A general handyman and cook's helper.

Bunker C: The type of oil used to fire steam locomotives.

Bunks: *See Log Bunks.*

Camp: A permanent or temporary working and living center in the woods.

Camp Car: A rail car used as working or living quarters.

Center Beam: The center sill which connects the two sets of trucks on a skeleton car.

Cheese Blocks: Lengths of iron forged into a triangular shape and attached to skeleton cars, through which chains are threaded to secure the logs. The blocks are set into the cars by long pins so they can be easily removed when dumping logs.

Climax: A small geared locomotive. All but the earliest models had canted cylinders which drove a transverse crankshaft from which power was transmitted via shafts and gears to the axles.

Cold Deck: A pile of logs held in storage.

Compound Locomotive: A locomotive built with one or more high-pressure cylinders which exhaust steam into low-pressure cylinders, in effect using the steam twice. Many early articulated locomotives were built this way. See *Mallet*.

Consolidation: A locomotive with a 2-8-0 wheel arrangement.

Couplers: The appliances with which rail cars are hooked together.

Crotch Line: A makeshift crane consisting of tongs (for gripping a log) suspended from a long spreader bar. The bar is hung between a steam donkey's mainline cable and haul-back cable, and can be swung back and forth and raised and lowered as necessary to maneuver a log.

Crown Sheet: A heavy metal sheet separating the fire box from the boiler water.

Crummy: A caboose.

Disconnects: Also called *High Trucks*. Independent sets of trucks, used in pairs, forming a rail "car" by being set under either end of a span of logs chained onto them.

Dogs: Hooks or pins driven into logs so they can be tied together for skidding or rafting.

Dolbeer Donkey: Named after its inventor, a steam donkey characterized by spools with vertical shafts.

Donkey: See *Steam Donkey*.

Donkey Doctor: A mechanic who maintains steam donkeys.

Donkey Puncher: A crew member who operates a steam donkey.

Doubling the Hill: Splitting a train in two or more sections and taking each section of a hill separately when the full train is too much to haul.

Drag Bucket: A large bucket powered by a steam donkey, used for earth moving.

Drag Lines: The lines connecting a drag bucket to a steam donkey.

Drawbar: The connection between a locomotive and tender, sometimes used synonymously with *Coupler*.

Drivers: The large wheels, powered by the engine, that propel a locomotive.

Drum: The spool on a steam donkey winch that holds the cable.

Dump: See *Log Dump*.

End Hooks: L-shaped hooks used at either end of a log to load it onto a rail car.

Engine: Mechanism for converting steam energy into motion. Another term for *Locomotive*.

Faller: A logger who does the actual cutting of timber with an ax and saw.

Fire Box: the part of a locomotive that houses the fire used to generate steam.

Flats: Flat cars. Rail cars with no sides on them.

Fore-and-Aft Road: See *Skid Road*.

Gandy Dancer: A track maintenance crew member.

Geared Locomotive: A steam locomotive whose wheels are driven by gears and shafts rather than by the more conventional system of rods directly connecting the pistons to drivers.

Glass: A small glass tube mounted vertically inside the cab to indicate the water level in the boiler. "A full glass of water" means the boiler is full.

Gons: Gondola cars.

Ground Man: A crew member who directs the crane operator from the ground.

Growler: A diesel-powered locomotive.

Haul Back: The line attached to a steam donkey which pulls the main line back toward the donkey.

Head End: The front end of a train.

Heisler: A geared locomotive characterized by a pair of cylinders mounted in a transverse "V" under the boiler.

Hickey: A heavy metal bar with a square hole in one end, used to set the brakes on disconnects and also as an aid in turning brake wheels.

Highclimber: A logger who climbs up and "tops" or cuts a tree to prepare it for use as a spar tree.

High Lead: The main line running between spar trees that carries the block and tackle attached to logs.

High Trucks: Another term for *Disconnects*.

Hog: A locomotive.

Hogger: A locomotive engineer.

Hole: The area between rail cars for the brakeman to stand while setting link-and-pin couplers.

Hostler: A locomotive caretaker. He fires up the engine in the morning and gets it ready for the engineer to take out on its day's run.

Hot Box: A fire caused by friction in a journal box.

Idler: An empty car placed between a locomotive's tender and the first load of timber, which acts as a spacer for safety,

Idler Trucks: Sets of disconnects used as a safety spacer. See *Idler*.

Jacket: The outside covering of a locomotive boiler.

Jammer: See *Steam Jammer*.

Jillpoke: A large pole mounted horizontally next to the track at a log dump. It is positioned at a diagonal so that, as a rail car approaches, the jillpoke will gradually push the logs off the car and into the water. It is then swung out of the way and repositioned as another car approaches.

Johnson Bar: The reverse lever on a locomotive.

Journal Box: The metal housing around the end of a rail car's axle, containing the bearings and lubricant.

Lead Trucks: Also called *Bogeys* or *Bogey Wheels*. The small wheels at the front of a locomotive.

Lead Lines: Another term for *High Lead*.

Link and Pin: A very early coupler design consisting of a link connecting two rail cars by means of a large iron pin slipped vertically through a hole in each end.

Loader: A device for loading logs onto rail cars.

Locking Dogs: Long vertical arms placed at the four corners of a flat car, used to keep logs from rolling off. The arms are hinged at the bottom so they fall away for easier unloading of logs.

Log Bunks: The part of a rail car which actually supports the weight of the logs.

Log Dump: The place at or near a mill at which logs are unloaded from rail cars.

Log Splash Dump: A dam built across a river to facilitate floating logs downstream. Water and logs build up behind the dam; then it is opened up, providing a thrust of water which moves the logs quickly and with enough depth to prevent them from becoming mired in shallow water.

Lokey: A steam locomotive.

Main Line: The primary railroad line from the mill to the woods, from which all spurs radiate. Also, the main cable of a steam donkey.

Mallet: (pronounced "malley"): Named after its inventer, a compound locomotive having two sets of drivers articulated under one boiler.

Mikado: A locomotive with a 2-8-2 wheel arrangement.

Mike: Nickname for Mikado.

Mogul: A locomotive with a 2-6-0 wheel arrangement

Parbuckle: A cable run under a log and pulled back over the top. By reeling in the upper end, a steam donkey could roll the log about. The method was usually used for loading logs onto cars.

Peavey: A wooden pole, steel-pointed at one end with a steel hook near the end. By sinking the point and hook into a log, the pole acts as a lever to maneuver logs.

Pole Road: See *Skid Road.*

Pot: Also called Steam Pot. A steam locomotive.

Prairie: A locomotive with a 2-6-2 wheel arrangement.

Priming: Priming the water injector to siphon water from the tender to the boiler.

Railhead: The point at which the track ends.

Reload: A location at which logs are transferred from one carrier to another, such as from overland trucks to rail or from a spur train to the main line.

Rigging: The cables and block and tackles used in maneuvering and loading logs.

Road: Railroad.

Roadbed: The prepared base on which track is laid.

Road Engine: A mainline locomotive (as opposed to a switcher or small spur engine).

Rod Engine: A conventional steam engine propelled by exterior rods connecting the pistons to the drivers.

Rooster: A wood or rail tongue linking a pair of disconnects beneath the load, as a safety device to prevent the trucks from being yanked out from under logs as the locomotive started to move.

Sand Dome: A dome-shaped compartment on top of a locomotive, holding sand which can be dispensed through piping to the rail for better traction.

Saturated Steam: Water heated to the point where it vaporizes and remains in saturated form while in contact with the water from which it was generated. Older locomotives were powered by this method.

Scaler: A string of disconnects positioned so they line up with their brakewheels on the same side. The brakeman could then walk alongside the train and set the brakes of each high truck without having to cross the track.

Sets: A string of disconnects positioned so they line up with their brakewheels on the same side. The brakeman could then walk alongside the train and set the brakes of each high truck without having to cross the track.

Shay: Manufactured by Lima Locomotive Works, a geared engine characterized by two or three adjacent cylinders, mounted vertically on the engine's right side, with fore-and-aft universally-jointed shafts transmitting power through bevel gears to the axles. When Lima's patent expired, the Willamette Iron & Steel Company manufactured copies of the engine. Though technically it could no longer be called a Shay, the distinction was rarely made in common usage.

Show: A logging operation.

Side Tank Locomotive: A locomotive with water tanks mounted horizontally outside the boiler and a small fuel bunker behind the cab, thus eliminating the need for a separate tender.

Sidewinder: Nickname for a Shay locomotive.

Simple Locomotive: An articulated locomotive designed so both sets of cylinders receive equal steam pressure, rather than high-pressure rear cylinders exhausting steam to low-pressure front cylinders. See *Compound Locomotive.*

Skeleton Car: A rail car used for transporting logs, consisting of a massive wooden or steel "backbone" running the length of the car, with a pair of chocks at each end to prevent the bottom row of logs from rolling off.

Skidder: A steam-powered logging machine equipped with winches and pulleys, used to drag cut timber. Unlike the steam donkey, whose cables were attached to a spar tree, the skidder had its own tower for pulleys and cables.

Skidding: The practice of dragging logs, usually by oxen or steam donkey.

Skid Road: Also called *Pole Road* or *Fore-and-Aft Road.* A trough made from logs set end-to-end on the ground. Wet, muddy, and peeled of bark, the logs form a slippery base on which to slide or "skid" felled timber from the logging area to the river.

Slobber Stack: A steam locomotive which blew an

excessive amount of grime out of her stack. These were usually earlier saturated steam type locomotives as opposed to the later superheated models which produced "drier" steam.

Spar Tree: A tall tree around which cables are attached for hauling logs out of the woods and loading them onto rail cars. A 200-foot tree can support about 1,000 feet of cable. Some of these same trees also provided spars for ships.

Speeder: A self-powered diesel rail car used for transporting crews.

Spiker: A member of a track-laying crew, who drives spikes to hold the rail onto the ties.

Spool Loader: A steam donkey whose spools for cable have vertical rather than horizontal shafts.

Spot: Nickname for engine numbers one through ten. For example, "the Two-spot" would be engine No. 2.

Squirrel Tails at the Pops: A fan of steam coming from a locomotive pop valve, which is opened when steam builds up too much pressure in the boiler.

Stack Talk: The chuffing sound made as steam exhausts through the smokestack of a locomotive; the heavier the load, the shorter and more pronounced the sound.

Steam Donkey: A steam-powered winch with a vertical boiler, used to drag felled timber to a waiting rail car.

Steamer: A steam locomotive.

Steam Jam: A steam operated locomotive brake, in lieu of the more modern air-operated brakes.

Sticks: Logs or railroad ties.

Superheated Steam: Water vapor heated to higher temperatures than saturated steam. Superheated steam is "drier" and produces 25-30% more power from the same amount of fuel. Most locomotives built after 1910 used this method.

Swamper: A crew member who cleans the engines and is also a general locomotive handyman.

Swing Donkey: Used in combination with one or more additional steam donkeys to maneuver logs about a storage yard.

Switcher: A small locomotive used primarily in rail yards for moving rail cars around, or for any type of chore not requiring heavy locomotive power.

Tallowpot: A fireman on a steam locomotive.

Tank Mallet: See *Side Tank Locomotive.*

Tender: The car immediately behind a steam locomotive, containing water for steam, and wood or oil for fuel.

Ten Wheeler: A locomotive with a 4-6-0 wheel arrangement.

Trailing Trucks: Also called *Bogeys* or *Bogey Wheels.*

The small wheels under the cab of a locomotive, used to support the weight of the firebox.

Trainmaster: The person in charge of all train movements; he gives orders to the various dispatchers and reports directly to the superintendent.

Trucks: The wheel assemblies of locomotive and rail cars.

Truss Rods: Steel rods suspended across posts which extend downward from a car's frame, to help prevent the frame from sagging under heavy loads. Truss rods preceded one-piece cast steel trusses.

Turn: Logs brought out of the woods in a single pull either by steam donkey, train or transport truck.

Walschaerts: A type of valve gear on a rod engine, named after its inventor.

Wheel Arrangement: The number of a locomotive's leading trucks, drivers, and trailing trucks, set off by hyphens, such as "2-6-2."

Whistle Punk: A crew member, usually a newcomer, whose job it is to whistle signals to others.

Yarder: A crew member in charge of steam donkey operations in the loading area of a logging camp.

Yarding: The process of hauling felled timber into a loading area. □

(Ken Schmelzer collection)

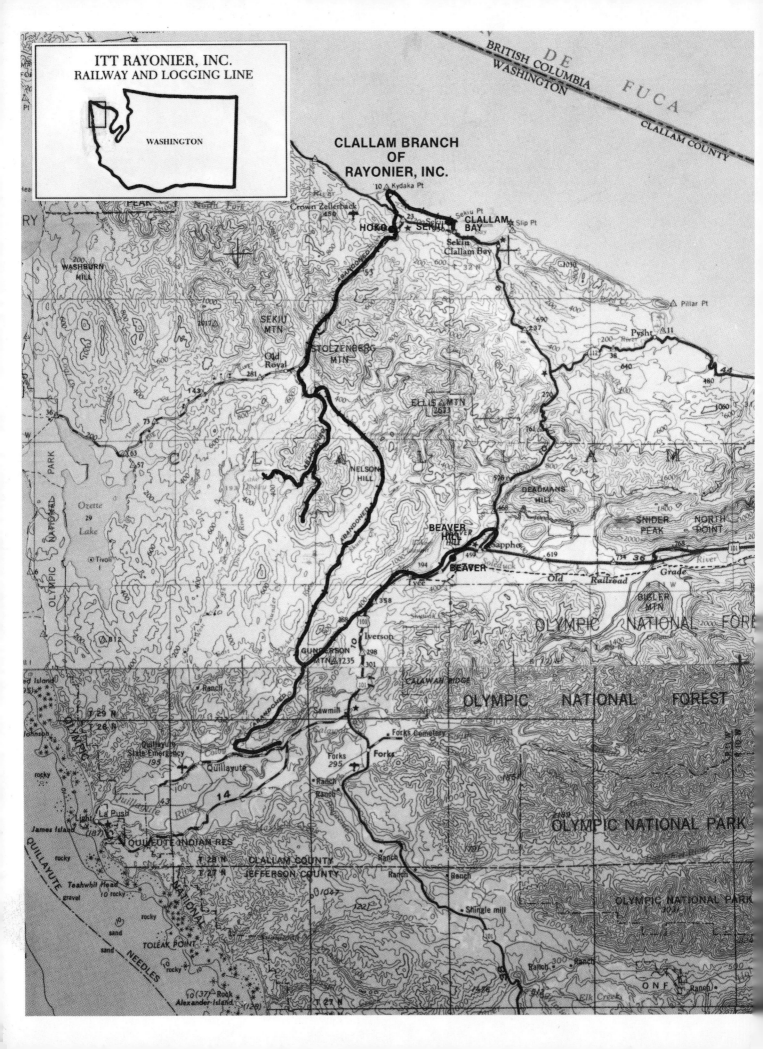